REAL-TIME SYSTEM SECURITY

REAL-TIME SYSTEM SECURITY

BRETT TJADEN AND
LONNIE R. WELCH (EDITORS)

Nova Science Publishers, Inc.
New York

Senior Editors: Susan Boriotti and Donna Dennis
Coordinating Editor: Tatiana Shohov
Office Manager: Annette Hellinger
Graphics: Wanda Serrano
Editorial Production: Vladimir Klestov, Matthew Kozlowski and Maya Columbus
Circulation: Ave Maria Gonzalez, Vera Popovic, Luis Aviles, Melissa Diaz,
     and Jeannie Pappas
Communications and Acquisitions: Serge P. Shohov
Marketing: Cathy DeGregory

Library of Congress Cataloging-in-Publication Data
Available upon request

ISBN 1-59033-586-4

Printed in the United States of America

CONTENTS

FOREWORD

In the early years of computing, real-time systems consisted of single computers interfaced to a few sensors and effectors, and perhaps to a user control device as well. The computer program in this processor almost certainly performed a cyclic closed loop control function, monitoring sensor inputs and commanding effectors in accord with a fixed and rigid control algorithm to achieve designer objectives such as managing process flow, vehicle motion, automatic response, etc.

While such systems still exist – and indeed have become almost ubiquitous in a myriad of everyday devices, including automobiles, appliances, spacecraft and video games – the world of real-time computing has expanded in scope and complexity in ways comparable to the proliferation of computers for many other aspects of business, economic and social life. Perhaps the most recent evidence of this expansion is the employment of distributed processing to achieve the objectives of real-time system designers.

With the expanded use of computers, particularly in distributed real-time embedded systems (DREs), issues of complexity have emerged that were not faced by early real-time system designers. It is true that small cyclic closed loop control systems are still built according to principles developed early in the history of real-time systems. Furthermore, in recent decades rate monotonic analysis (RMA) has provided a theoretical underpinning for such systems, but the actual architectural structure has changed little.

On the other hand, complex aggregations of computers operating as a distributed system have assumed a distinctly different character from early real-time systems, exhibiting far more variation in form as well as in the underlying technology base. Dealing with this complexity has become a major driver for innovation in both system architecture and computing technology. The challenge designers face today is, how to design, build, deploy and maintain ever larger and more capable distributed real-time embedded systems to meet the demands of a changing world.

Furthermore, the traditional problems of functionality and performance are seriously compounded because such systems can no longer be optimized exclusively for performance but instead must find a suitable niche in a complexity, multi-dimensional trade space involving many design factors, including real-time performance, survivability, secure operation, large size, complex, long service life, continuous evolution, distribution, mission criticality, and cost consciousness. In summary, modern real-time systems are likely to be more than just systems; they are rapidly becoming large-scale systems of systems.

Because of their long life and high cost, complex real-time systems cannot be recreated as new starts when new requirements emerge. They must evolve and undergo changes and upgrades in place. Furthermore, since the technology base on which DREs are built is changing rapidly, complex real-time systems must allow for the convenient insertion of new computing equipment and supporting software products. For these reasons, flexibility of design has become a paramount concern.

Technical Characteristics

Technically, real-time systems encompass a wide range of characteristics that fundamentally impact their design and operation. No longer are they relatively straightforward cyclic hard real-time programs. They must deal with and accommodate a wide variety of processing objectives. These include:

- Driven by external world events
- External environments that cannot be characterized accurately a priori
- High volume throughput of continuously refreshed data
- Hard real-time deadline aperiodics
- Asynchronous, event-based low latency responses
- Soft real-time processing requirements
- Reaction time paths across multiple hardware and software components
- Wide dynamic range of processing loads
- Operator display and control requirements
- High availability and survivability requirements
- Stringent certification and safety requirementsOpen Systems

Given the rapidity with which commercial computing technology is evolving, a major consideration for any long-lived system is the problem of efficiently changing the underlying COTS (commercial-off-the-shelf) computing technology at frequent intervals to keep it current and easily maintainable. This process is often referred to as *technology refresh*. A fundamental problem arises in performing this process when application code is tightly coupled to the underlying technology base and that base changes frequently in ways that impact application code.

In such circumstances, the implementation of a technology refresh also necessitates revision and retesting of the application computer programs. In worst case circumstances, the time and cost to accomplish this exercise may constitute a significant percentage of the original development cost of the system – while providing no increase in functionality or performance. Clearly, this is an unacceptable situation, especially given the sums of money involved. Methods for reducing this cost are very much in demand.

The method that has evolved within the DRE community involves a combination of using standards-based hardware and support software combined with extensive layering of modest sized componentized software products, each one of which isolates the layers above from changes below via standard or pseudo-standard application programmer interfaces (APIs). Systems built according to this approach are called *open systems*. Such systems are easy to upgrade and to refresh because hardware and support software components on which applications reside are, by design, interoperable and interchangeable. In its POSIX documentation, IEEE defines an open system as:

> *A system that implements sufficient open specifications for interfaces, services, and supporting formats to enable properly engineered applications software: (a) to be ported with minimal changes across a wide range of systems, (b) to interoperate with other applications on local and remote systems, and (c) to interact with users in a style that facilitates user portability.*

Open systems – and architectures built according to open system principles – possess a number of common characteristics. While not every open system possesses every possible characteristic, most open systems tend to possess most of these characteristics. The attributes of an open system include the following:

- Use of public, consensus-based standards
- Adoption of standard interfaces
- Adoption of standard services (defined functions)
- Use of product types supported by multiple vendors
- Selection of stable vendors with broad customer bases and large market shares
- Interoperability, with minimal integration
- Ease of scalability and upgradability
- Portability of application(s)
- Portability of users

The result of incorporating open system principles into a system architecture is that such systems fulfill the following relationship:

Open Systems = Standard Interfaces + Defined Capability → Interoperability + Ease of Change

While devising rigorous metrics that reflect abstract concepts such as open systems and open architecture is difficult, it is not impossible – especially as long as one realizes that such metrics may themselves be somewhat qualitative. For example, standards compliance may be approximated by first-order estimation of the ratio of standards-based APIs to total APIs. Time and work effort needed to incorporate new functions may be tracked and compared to historical data about similar activities. Numbers of interfaces, especially multi-client server interfaces, may be compared to previous implementations. Early process-oriented system engineering efforts should address this question explicitly.

Managing Change

In virtually all long-lived systems, change is inevitable, and usually occurs at many levels. Application functions change, paced by threats and missions. Computing technology changes, driven by technological innovation and market pressures. Even standards change, albeit at a slower pace. Managing this change and isolating its effects is the key to successful implementation of DREs. The primary techniques for attaining isolation are use of standards, and use of a category of support software known as middleware.

Middleware comes in two major types, adaptation middleware and distribution middleware. A third type of support software, resource management, provides system management functions that are not strictly middleware in nature but that, like adaptation and distribution middleware, provide vital services in the composition of large systems.

Together, these three types of support software provide a synthesizing function that allows applications in a distributed system to interface with each other and with the underlying computing equipment and operating systems.

System Flexibility

In the past, systems, both distributed and otherwise, have been designed with a fixed and rigid allocation of processing tasks to processing resources – i.e., in a manner somewhat analogous to the fixed and rigid time division multiplexing approach of real-time cyclic computer programs and executives. This approach has many advantages, not the least of which is its analyzability and predictability. It is, in a relative sense, easy to design, build and test.

However, this approach also has weaknesses, just as the cyclic approach to real-time computation has weaknesses. In the case of a fixed allocation of processing to processing resources, the weaknesses include a similar brittleness of design, a fault tolerance approach that generally requires at least double the amount of equipment as that required to simply provide inherent mission functionality, and an inflexibility in operation that substantially inhibits run time adaptation to the dynamic conditions of the moment.

Such systems are also frequently constrained in their performance by design choices made at system inception and early design. In particular, many systems exhibit a performance "sweet spot" where they perform well. When pressed to operate beyond this range in terms of capacity requirements, they tend to degrade in performance, sometimes catastrophically. In effect, such designs are not scalable with respect to system load. The application code needed to manage load shedding in such circumstances adds significantly to development cost, test time and software defects.

One of the best examples of the impact of lack of scalability is that of the popular Internet service provider, America Online. Years ago, AOL changed its pricing structure from a use-time basis to a fixed fee per month. Not unexpectedly (except to AOL management), users thus freed from the cost burden of time-based charges began staying online much longer. AOL had not anticipated this sudden increase in required capacity. Furthermore its architecture was not particularly scalable at that time. The result was a highly visible nation-wide gridlock for AOL users.

Dynamic Resource Management

It is interesting and significant that, at least in the web service market place, new technologies have since been developed to deal explicitly with the need to dynamically adapt to wide variations in service and capacity requirements placed on computing resources. These technological innovations encompass both hardware solutions and software solutions. In either case, their purpose is to provide system designers with a *dynamic resource management* capability.

Dynamic Resource Management, or DRM, is a computer system management capability that provides monitoring and control of network, computer, sensor, actuator, operating system, middleware, and application resources within a distributed computing environment. DRM is a critical component for exploiting the new computing capabilities emerging from the rapidly evolving COTS technology sector. When combined with a standards-based and modular approach to system design, DRM provides an ability to readily change system configurations to support not only rapid insertion of new functional algorithms but also rapid and inexpensive COTS technology refresh.

Without DRM and without the portability that an open systems approach fosters, each insertion of new functional capability and each change out of COTS computing equipment must be accomplished via a lengthy redesign and development process, with their inherent cost and schedule impact.

The primary unique capability provided by Resource Management is its ability to maintain a user specified level of performance for each application computer program as it executes on the available computer system resources. DRM accomplishes this function by allocating – and reallocating as necessary – the application computer programs to the computer resources based on the ongoing observed performance of the application system as it operates and performs its designed functions. Once the application system has been initially allocated and initiated, DRM maintains the user specified level of performance in the presence of not only changing a computer system configuration (e.g., due to computer and/or network failures) but also varying external stimuli experienced by the application system and changing mission requirements as designated by the application system's users.

Because of this flexible dynamic allocation capability, DRM confers a number of benefits on real-time systems. DRM is particularly valuable for mission critical systems that must maintain a specified level of performance, the absence of which may lead to drastic, even catastrophic consequences.

DRM provides three major system benefits. First, it allows the DRE system to sustain a level of performance that is invariant with respect to external load. By allocating computing resources to critical computations that would otherwise be overloaded, a steady level of performance is maintained. Second, since the system resource allocation can be rebalanced during system operation, the system can be tuned to the mission at hand. Thus, mission flexibility is conferred, a capability which is virtually unknown today.

Finally, because the DRM capability treats the entire computing system as a pool of computers, any one of which can run any program, any computer can serve as a backup or spare for fault tolerance. Thus, rather than a primary-backup fault tolerance model, the proper view in a DRM-managed system is an N + M redundancy scheme. This approach has the potential to drastically increase operational availability following casualty events.

For systems where maintenance of the deployed system is a concern, DRM offers an additional benefit. DRM acts as a manning reduction and operational cost saving enabler. Use of the pool of computers approach means that any computer can do any function (with certain specialized exceptions). This in turn means that if a sufficiently large pool of computers is incorporated into the pool by design, computers that fail during deployment do not have to be maintained at sea but instead can be repaired or replaced upon return to port. This in turn means that personnel do not have to be dedicated to computer system maintenance, thus reducing maintenance staffing and operational cost.

Building Real-time Open Architectures

In broad and general terms, architecture is defined as "the structural design of an entity." Adding "openness" to the list of architectural characteristics implies that the "structure" of the architecture explicitly promotes interoperability, both internally and externally, as well as ease of modification and extension.

It is an engineering truism that what is achievable in system design (architecture) is a function of not only the task to be accomplished but also the technologies that are available. In the early days of real-time computing, the technology base included custom or niche market computers, point-to-point connectivity, real-time executives and a variety of proprietary support packages tailored to the specific characteristics of individual applications.

However, the evolution of high performance COTS provides an opportunity to design architectures capable of meeting the demands of ever more complex and demanding applications. The need for evolution of architecture toward an open and distributed approach is motivated by both performance and supportability considerations. Commensurate with this dual set of motivating factors, the goals of open architectures are as follows:

- DREs that continue to meet their mission needs through upgrades and changes
- System design that fosters affordable development and life cycle maintenance
- System design that reduces upgrade cycle time and time-to-deployment for new features
- Architecture that is technology refreshable despite rapid COTS obsolescence

Finally, note that system requirements include not only capability and performance goals but also engineering "-ility" goals as well. In addition to traditional "-ilities" such as reliability and survivability, the "-ilities" of open architectures include metrics such as *portability, affordability, extensibility* and *flexibility of use*. These objectives are met, in part, with careful design and in part through use of open systems principles and standards. In many cases, the best design choices and technologies are those that support these latter "-ilities" as well as traditional measures such as performance and functionality.

Michael W. Masters
U.S. Naval Surface Warfare Center,
Dahlgren Division;
MastersMW@nswc.navy.mil
Lonnie R. Welch
School of EECS,
Ohio University;
welch@ohio.edu

PREFACE

Mission critical real-time systems often function in environments that cannot be modeled with static approaches. Because of their (externally-driven) wide dynamic range of system operation, the number of data elements to be processed in an arbitrary period is unknown at the time of system engineering (other than an extremely pessimistic worst case sense). While it may be possible to determine a theoretical upper bound on the number of data items, the construction and maintenance of system components to handle worst-case conditions can be prohibitively costly. To accommodate such dynamic mission critical real-time systems, it is useful to design computing systems that allow reconfiguration and reallocation of resources by sharing a pool of distributed computational resources. Unfortunately, the problem of continuously providing critical system functions in such dynamic real-time environments is exacerbated when one considers attack vulnerability. The Internet has made mission critical real-time computer systems subject to an ever-changing array of attacks for which current defense mechanisms are insufficient. In order to combat intruders in this new environment, new techniques must be developed that enable decision makers to *detect* unusual behavior in their systems, *correlate* anomalies into higher-level attacker goals, *plan* appropriate response actions, and *execute* their plans. This special issue presents current work in this general area of *real-time system security*.

Balupari et al. present their work on INBOUNDS (Integrated Network-Based Ohio University Network Detective Service), a network based anomaly detection system. INBOUNDS is built atop Real-Time TCPTrace, a network traffic capture and analysis program. Real-Time TCPTrace reports every opened and closed network connection, and, periodically, it provides statistics on the activity of all currently opened connections. From this data, INBOUNDS automatically builds profiles of each different network service that it sees. In detection mode, INBOUNDS compares the statistics for an ongoing connection with the profile for the corresponding service to identify connections that are behaving abnormally. INBOUNDS' primary goal is to detect newly developed attacks or variants on existing attacks that are not easily recognized by existing intrusion detection systems.

Jiang et al. discuss a scheme for padding network traffic in an ad-hoc wireless network to limit the amount of useful information an intruder can discern though traffic analysis. Ad-hoc wireless networks possess several unique characteristics that can be valuable in mission critical real-time systems, however, poor security and constraints on energy consumption have limited their deployment in such environments. Jiang et al. propose traffic padding through the insertion of dummy traffic to camouflage the communication patterns present in the real traffic. Further, their scheme attempts to minimize the amount of dummy traffic used in order to reduce the overhead in terms of energy required per unit of real traffic delivered.

Chappell et al. describe the information security environment faced by the U.S. Navy. Mission critical applications that have hard real-time requirements are described. The types of systems discussed range from geographically dispersed operational sites which may have timing constraints in the range of seconds, to shipboard combat system that are responsible for threat assessment, command and control, and targeting weapons which must operate well below the one second threshold. Chappell explains how he and his colleagues at the Naval Surface Warfare Center have begun evaluating the applicability of Intrusion Detection Systems (IDS) in naval environments. Included in this discussion are the current security architectures of naval platforms, some potential future architectures, and the desirable features for intrusion detection systems that may be integrated into these architectures in the future.

Lim et al. address the emerging trend towards connecting distributed embedded devices and the challenges of ensuring integrity and service availability in such an environment. They point to the notion of "smart home" with many embedded devices, which have a simple web interface. Compared with traditional desktop systems, these embedded devices have certain advantages in terms of security, especially since embedded devices do not typically allow remote login, or support emails with attachments. Nevertheless, most embedded devices will accept downloadable code from the Internet in order to enable product support and upgrades. This mobile code is a substantial security risk, and the authors talk in their paper about the risks associated with accepting questionable control source code for embedded "smart" devices.

Li and Ye present their decision tree techniques that can be used to automatically identify intrusion signatures, and to subsequently classify activities in computer network systems as either normal or intrusive. They demonstrate how to design and build decision tree classifiers using different feature selection methods such as "single event," "moving window," "EWMA vector," and "state ID." Taking training and testing data from the audit data supplied by the Basic Security Module of the Solaris operating system, they present the performance of their decision tree classifiers under several different conditions.

Brett Tjaden and Lonnie Welch
Ohio University, Athens, USA

REAL-TIME NETWORK-BASED ANOMALY INTRUSION DETECTION

RAVINDRA BALUPARI, BRETT TJADEN, SHAWN OSTERMANN, MARINA
BYKOVA, AARON MITCHELL*

Abstract. The global internet has made computer systems world-wide vulnerable to an ever-changing array of attacks. A new approach to perform real-time network-based anomaly intrusion detection is presented in this paper. Real-time Tcptrace generates data streams which are analysed to detect network-based attacks. Real-time Tcptrace periodically reports statistics on all the open TCP/IP connections in the network. Then, using the Abnormality Factor method, statistical profiles are built for the normal behavior of the network services. Abnormal activity is then flagged as an intrusion. This approach has the advantage of being able to monitor any service without the prior knowledge of modelling its behavior. The paper presents interesting results and evaluation of the approach by conducting experiments using the MIT Lincoln lab evaluation data.

Keywords – Anomaly intrusion detection, Real-time Tcptrace, Abnormality Factor method, statistical profiles, data streams, dimensions, services, abnormal behavior.

1. Introduction. The Internet was originally conceived of and designed as a research and education network, but the usage patterns have changed radically. It has become a home for private and commercial communication, commerce, medicine, and public service. Increased reliance on the Internet is expected, along with increased attention to its security. In the face of the vulnerabilities and the consequences of intrusion in computer network systems, a robust and flexible defense strategy is required that allows adaptation to the changing environment, well-defined policies and procedures, use of robust tools, and constant vigilance. Efforts in this direction led to the development of Intrusion Detection Systems.

In this paper,we present a new approach to perform real-time network-based anomaly intrusion detection as a part of the INBOUNDS(Integrated Network-Based Ohio University Network Detective Service) system. This approach detects suspicious behavior by scrutinizing network data obtained from Real-time Tcptrace. The use of Real-time Tcptrace is the major distinction between our approach and the approach taken by existing intrusion detection systems. IN-BOUNDS is designed to function in a heterogenous environment with very low overhead, and high degree of scalability.This paper describes the architecture of INBOUNDS and provides a detailed description of our approach to anomaly intrusion detection. This paper also assesses our approach and presents our results to date.

2. Related Work. In 1987, Dorothy Denning [4] presented the idea that intrusions in computer systems could be detected by assuming that users of a

*School of Electrical Engineering and Computer Science, Ohio University, Athens, OH 45701 (rbalupar|tjaden|osterman|mbykova|amitchel@cs.ohiou.edu).

computer system would behave in a manner that would lend itself to automatic profiling. Some of the first IDSs to implement Denning's vision were the Intrusion Detection Expert System (IDES) [9] and the Multics Intrusion Detection and Alerting System (MIDAS) [16]. These systems were host based and scrutinized the audit data for occurences of known intrusive behavior. The move from standalone to networked computer systems motivated the development of multihost-based IDS. Stalker [18], for example, was a successor of the host based system named Haystack [17]. Both these systems perform off-line misuse detection on a group of hosts using a centralized monitoring station. Many real-time, multihost based intrusion detection systems were also developed. Adaptive Intrusion Detection System (AID) [20] was developed at Brandenburg University of Technology, Germany, and was used to detect system misuse in a heterogeneous UNIX environment. The Distributed Intrusion Detestion System (DIDS) [19] is another mutlihost based, real-time intrusion detection system that features "distributed monitoring and data reduction with centralized data analysis". There are a number of other mutlihost based, real-time, centralized systems including the Next-generation Intrusion Detection Expert System (NIDES) [1] by SRI International, the Information Security Officer's Assistant (ISOA) [23] by Planning Research Corporation, and the Computer Misuse Detection System (CMDS) [15] by Science Applications International Corporation. Distributed, multihost based, real-time intrusion detection systems include the Cooperating Security Monitor (CSM) [22], developed at Texas A & M University and Purdue's Autonomous Agents for Intrusion Detection (AAFID) [24].

As computing moved to a distributed environment, a number of network-based intrusion detection systems were developed. Los Alamos National Laboratories' Network Anomaly Detection and Intrusion Reporter (NADIR) [7] performs off-line anomaly detection on a large network of supercomputers running the UNICOS operating system, and has been recently updated to UNICORN [3] which operates in real-time. Distributed real-time network-based intrusion detection systems are still in the early research stage of development. The Graph Based Intrusion Detection System (GrIDS) [2] by the University of California, Davis and SRI International's Event Monitoring Enabling Repsponses to Anomalous Live Disturbances (EMERALD) [11] SRI and our own INBOUNDS are three such systems.

3. The INBOUNDS Architecture. INBOUNDS, the Integrated Network-Based Ohio University Network Detective Service, is a realtime intrusion detection system being developed at Ohio University. The INBOUNDS system detects suspicious behavior by scrutinizing network and host data gathered from various data sources. It is a network-based, real-time, centralized intrusion detection system that performs anomaly detection. Designed to function in large distributed real-time environment, the goals of the INBOUNDS system are to: run continually, be fault tolerant, resist subversion, be scalable, operate with minimal overhead, be easily configurable, cope with changing system behavior, be difficult to fool and, most importantly, to detect never before seen attacks. As shown in Fig 3.1, the INBOUNDS system consists of the Data Collection, Current Data Repository, Historical Data Respository, Data Visualization and Intrusion Detection components.

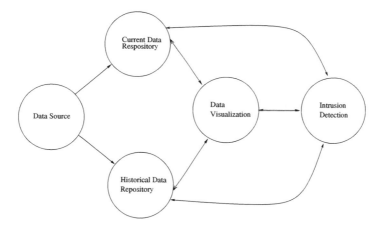

FIG. 3.1. *INBOUNDS Architecture*

3.1. Data Collection. The Data Collection component provides the source of the data that is used by the other components in INBOUNDS. Data collection is performed by a group of modules that capture, filter, process and summarize information about the networks, hosts, users, processes, and resources of a dynamic, distributed system. Each data source produces a real-time stream of information that flows optionally through a filter and then to the Current and Historical Data Repositories. The most important data source for INBOUNDS is Real-time Tcptrace [10], which provides information about network traffic. Other data sources include DeSiDeRaTa [21] host monitors, which report host and resource utilization statistics.

3.1.1. Real-time Tcptrace:. Real-time Tcptrace is an extension to Tcptrace [10], a widely used network traffic analysis tool created by Dr. Shawn Ostermann at Ohio University. Tcptrace [10] reads dump files collected by any one of several popular packet capturing programs like Tcpdump, Snoop, Ehterpeek and Netm. It groups packets into conversations, and performs analysis of individual or groups of conversations. One type of analysis performed includes detecting re-transmissions, calculating round trip times and measuring throughput. Real-time Tcptrace is implemented by adding a new module that gathers information about network activity and reports it in real-time. It provides information about new connections that are being opened and old connections that are being closed. Real-time Tcptrace also reports periodically, statistics on all exisiting connections during that time interval.

Every time a new connection is opened, Real-time Tcptrace generates a message reporting the time at which the connection was opened, the source and destination IP [5] addresses and port numbers of the connection, and the manner in which the connection was opened. The format of the open connection message Real-time Tcptrace sends to INBOUNDS is as follows:
$O < time\_stamp >< src\_addr >:< src\_port >< dst\_addr >:< dst\_port ><$ $status >$ where,

- O: Identifies the message as open connection message.
- $< time\_stamp >$: time stamp on the packet opening the connection.
- $< status >$: field to specify the status of the open connection.
  - 0 - connection was opened with a SYN [6] packet.
  - 1 - connection was established previously.

Real-time Tcptrace assumes that the packet that initiates the connection is a "question". All the packets that travel in the same direction as the initial packet are considered questions, and packets travelling in the other direction are "answers". At set intervals (currently every 60 seconds), Real-time Tcptrace reports statistics on all currently opened connections. The statistics, also called dimensions of a connection, reported are:

- *Interactivity:* number of questions during the time interval normalized to 1 second.
- *ASOQ:* average size of questions during the time interval in bytes.
- *ASOA:* average size of answers during the time interval in bytes.
- *QAIT:* sum of idle question-answer time during the time interval normalized to 1 second.
- *AQIT:* sum of idle answer-question time during the time interval normalized to 1 second.

Figure 3.2 illustrates a connection between a Client and a Server. The connection between the time interval from T1 to T2 is shown. During this period the client sends three questions while the server replies with three answers. From the illustration,

- the Interactivity of the connection during the time interval from T1 to T2 will be, $Interactivity = 3/(T2 - T1)$ questions/sec
- The average size of questions during the time interval from T1 to T2 will be, $ASOQ = (Sizeof(Q1) + Sizeof(Q2) + Sizeof(Q3))/3$ bytes
- The average size of answers during the time interval from T1 to T2 will be, $ASOA = (Sizeof(A1) + Sizeof(A2) + Sizeof(A3))/3$ bytes
- The sum of idle question-answer time during the time interval from T1 to T2 will be, $QAIT = (QAT1 + QAT2 + QAT3)/(T2 - T1)$ sec/sec
- The sum of idle answer-question time during the time interval from T1 to T2 will be, $AQIT = (AQT1 + AQT2)/(T2 - T1)$ sec/sec

Real-time Tcptrace calculates these five dimensions for each existing connection and generates interactivity reports on open connections at set intervals. The format of these interactivity messages is as follows:
$I < time\_stamp >< src\_addr >:< src\_port >< dst\_addr >:< dst\_port ><$ $n1 >< n2 >< n3 >< n4 >< n5 >$

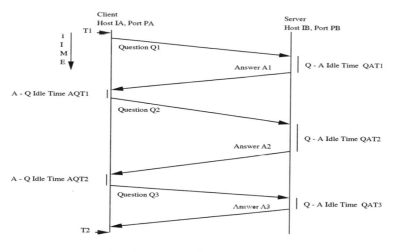

FIG. 3.2. *Client-Server connection*

where,
- I: Identifies the information as interactivity message.
- $< time\_stamp >$: time at which the information is generated.
- $< n1 >$:Interactivity (floating point number)
- $< n2 >$:ASOQ (floating point number)
- $< n3 >$:ASOA (floating point number)
- $< n4 >$:QAIT (floating point number)
- $< n5 >$:AQIT (floating point number)

When a connection is closed (or a half open connection is timed out), Real-time Tcptrace generates a close message, which contains many of the same fields as an open message:

$C < time\_stamp >< src\_addr >:< src\_port >< dst\_addr >:< dst\_port >< status >$

where,
- C: Identifies the message as closing message
- $< time\_stamp >$: time stamp on the packet closing the connection.
- $< status >$: field to specify the status of the closed connection.
  - 0 - connection was closed with two FIN [6] packets.
  - 1 - connection was reset by RST [6] packet.
  - 2 - half-open connection that was timed out.

The close message is preceded by an interactivity message for the closing connection, which provides the details of the five dimensions for that connection in the time interval prior to closing of connection.

The current implementation of Real-time Tcptrace uses Tcpdump to capture TCP/IP [6] packets over a switched ethernet network. Tcpdump is run on a host with port mirroring, which can capture all the packets on the network being monitored. Real-time Tcptrace currently does not provide information about connections established with UDP [12] packets or ICMP [13] packets.

3.2. Current Data Repository. The Current Data Repository(CDR) is a data storage component that provides current data to other components in the system. It accepts streams of data from various Data Collection modules and passes only the streams requested by the modules in the Visualization and Intrusion Detection components. The data that passes through the CDR is the most recent and detailed data in the system, Real-time Tcptrace open, close, and interactivity messages, for example. The modules in the Visualization and Intrusion Detection components register with the CDR to receive the type of data in which they are interested. CDR performs minimal buffering of the data streams received from the Data Collection module and ensures that no data is lost, and that it passes on the most recent data.

3.3. Historical Data Respository. The Historical Data Repository (HDR) is a data storage component that contains older and more coarse grained information. It provides this information for other modules in the INBOUNDS system upon request. The HDR accepts real-time data streams from the modules in the Data Collection and Intrusion Detection components. It abstracts the information, storing only a brief summary of the data stream. Pieces of information are explicitly requested from the HDR using a client-server model of interaction. For example, by interacting with the HDR an analysis module might learn the remote sites from which a user has connected in the past, the kinds of services and resources a user or site typically uses, and whether any site or user has engaged in suspicious behavior in the past.

3.4. Data Visualization. The Data Visualization component is intended to allow a human to view and make sense of the huge amount of current and historical data in the system. It provides an interface for the user to navigate between various levels of abstraction and provides different views of the data to discern interested information. It also provides the information about the intrusion events generated by the Intrusion Detection component. The Data Visualization component allows the user to configure and fine tune the INBOUNDS system. Currently this component is a graphical user interface designed using Java programming language.

3.5. Intrusion Detection. The Intrusion Detection component performs the task of analysing the data collected by the various data collection modules to detect intrusions. The following sections provide a detailed description of the design, implementation, and assessment of this module which performs real-time network-based anomaly intrusion detection using the network activity information obtained from Real-time Tcptrace.

4. Real-time Network-based Anomaly Intrusion Detection. The task of network-based anomaly intrusion detection in the INBOUNDS system is performed by the Network Anomaly Intrusion Detection (NAID) module. This module detects anomalous behavior and reports it in real-time. The idea behind the NAID module is to detect unusual behavior of the services on the hosts in a network. It builds statistical profiles of the five different dimensions during normal operation and watches for significant deviations from these profiles. The network activity is composed of the activity of a number of connections between different hosts in the network. This activity can be defined by using six dimensions, five of which characterize each connection and the sixth one characterizes all the connections. As discussed in Sect. 3.1.1, the five dimensions which characterize each connection are: Interactivity, ASOQ, ASOA, QAIT and AQIT. The sixth dimension is the Number of Connections(NOC) in the network.

4.0.1. NAID approaches:. The NAID module takes two different approaches to monitor the network activity using the dimensions described above. They are:

1. All Connections to All Hosts on a particular port(ACAH).
2. All Connections to a Single Host on a particular port(ACSH).

In the ACAH approach, the NAID module will monitor the behavior of a service on a specified port on all hosts in the network. It will look for abnormalities in the following dimensions for all the connections to all the hosts using that specified port: total Interactivity, total ASOQ, total ASOA, total QAIT, total AQIT, and total NOC. This enables INBOUNDS to detect if a particular service running on a port on all the hosts being monitored is behaving abnormally. For example, the SMTP [14] servers on port 25 of various machines will exhibit an abnormally large number of total connections(NOC) in the case of an e-mail macro virus. In such a case, each of the single connections on that particular port may have normal behavior, but overall analysis of all the connections will show anomalous behavior.

In the ACSH approach, the NAID module will monitor the behavior of all the connections to a specified port on a particular host in the network. It will look for abnormalities in the following dimensions for all the connections to the specified host: total Interactivity, total ASOQ, total ASOA, total QAIT, total AQIT, and total NOC. This enables INBOUNDS to detect if a particular service on a specific host has been compromised. For example, abnormally high interactivity would be exhibited by the finger deamon in the case of a buffer overflow attack.

4.0.2. NAID Statistical Method:. The NAID module utilizes Abnormality Factor(AF) method to monitor the behavior of the six dimensions for anomalies in the two approaches discussed above. In this method, the HDR is used to store the average and standard deviation values of certain dimensions for a particular key. The key can be a port number, a host IP [5] address, or a combination of both.

When a new set of values for a key are obtained from the Current Data Repository, the individual values of each dimension are compared to their respective average and standard deviation values obtained from the HDR. The standard deviation values are used to find the distance 'D' of the new value from the average value expressed as the number of standard deviations. A threshold called the Standardization Factor 'SF' is set and all the individual values which are at a distance 'D' less than or equal to Standardization Factor 'SF' are assigned an Abnormality Factor 'AF' equal to zero. When the distance 'D' is more than the Standardization Factor 'SF', the ceiling of the difference of distance 'D' and Standardization Factor 'SF' is assigned to Abnormality Factor 'AF'. For example, consider the dimension ASOQ (Average size of questions) for a key. At time T, the value of ASOQ obtained from the Current Data Repository is, $V = 35.47$ bytes. The values obtained from the Historical Data Repository are, Average $A = 20.01$ bytes and Standard deviation $SD = 3.12$. The distance of the dimension value from the average will be, $d = V - A = 35.47 - 20.01 = 15.46$ bytes. This distance is then expressed as the number of standard deviations, $D = d/SD = 15.46/3.12 = 4.96$. If the Standardization Factor is set to 2, $SF = 2$, then the distance D is more than SF, so Abnormality Factor will be, $AF = \lceil (D - SF) \rceil = 3$.

This procedure is used to determine the Abnormality Factor for each dimension for a given key. The sum of the Abnormality Factors of all the dimensions for that key is then compared against a pre-defined threshold value to detect any abnormalities. For example, consider that there are five dimensions: Interactivity, ASOQ, ASOA, QAIT and AQIT, being profiled for a key. At instant T, using the above described procedure the Abnormality Factors for each dimension are determined to be, AF(Interactivity) = 2, AF(ASOQ) = 3, AF(ASOA) = 0, AF(QAIT) = 3 and AF(AQIT) = 0. The sum of Abnormality Factors will be, AF(Sum) =(AF(Interactivity) + AF(ASOQ) + AF(ASOA) + AF(QAIT) + AF(AQIT)) = 8. If the pre-defined threshold value, $Th = 5$, then it can be seen that AF(sum) > Th and hence it can be determined that the key shows abnormal behavior at instant T.

4.1. ACAH approach using Abnormality Factor method. In the ACAH approach of monitoring the network using Abnormality Factor method, the NAID module uses HDR to compute and store the average and standard deviation values of the six dimensions for a particular port. The HDR is also used to store intrusion information generated by the module. The NAID module recieves the open, close and network activity information from the Current Data Repository. It processes only the data items which correspond to the network activity information of a connection.

$I < time\_stamp >< src\_addr >:< src\_port >< dst\_addr >:< dst\_port ><$ $n1 >< n2 >< n3 >< n4 >< n5 >$

The NAID module parses the interactivity message data stream and stores the information of the individual data fields. It then determines the smaller of the destination and source port numbers. The information of the individual data fields is then added to the previous information stored for that service(the smaller of the two port numbers). For example, when the NAID module receives the following data stream, I 920986006.364042 132.235.17.1:3405 132.235.15.1:25 1.679000 162.625000 32.750000 0.003470 0.005993, it will break the data stream into individual fields and stores the information. It then determines the smaller of the two port numbers, 25, as the server-port. The information of the individual fields of the data stream is then added to the previous information stored for the server-port 25. Similarly, all the interactivity messages about the currently open connections is used to update the information stored for the approproiate services.

After profile time period, the module has the information for every service that was involved in network activity. During this time period, the Total Interactivity of all the connections for a particular service is obtained by adding the individual interactivity values of each connection for that service. The values of the dimensions Total ASOQ, Total ASOA, Total QAIT and Total AQIT are obtained in a similar manner. The Total NOC is obtained by counting the number of connections present for that service during the time period.

The operation of the intrusion detection using the Abnormality Factor method of ACAH approach is performed by the NAID module after every profile time period. The Total dimension values of all the connections for a service are obtained using the above described procedure. The average and standard deviation values for the service are obtained from HDR. The Abnormality Factor (AF) for each dimensions is obtained using the Abnormality Factor method described in Sect. 4. The sum of these Abnormality Factors is then compared to a pre-defined threshold value to detect any abnormalities. In the case when the sum of the Abnormality Factors is more than the pre-defined threshold value an alert is generated. The alert indicates an abnormal activity in the network on that service during that profile time period. In case of an alert, the information of the individual connections causing the abnormality is stored in HDR. In the case when the sum of the Abnormality Factors is less than pre-defined threshold value, no alert is raised, and the total dimension values are passed to the HDR, which calculates and stores the new average and standard deviation values.

The process of comparision is done for all the services involved in communication in the network. When the communication on a service takes place for the first time, the total dimension values are directly sent to the HDR. All the information stored during the profile time period is cleared at the end of the comparisions and the process of detecting intrusions is repeated after every profile time period.

4.2. ACSH approach using Abnormality Factor method. In the ACSH approach of monitoring the network using the Abnormality Factor method, the NAID module uses HDR to store the average and the standard deviation values of the six dimensions for a key composed of the host IP [5] address and port number. The HDR is also used to store the intrusion information generated

by the module. The NAID module recieves the open, close and network activity information from Current Data Repository. It processes only the data items which correspond to the network activity information of a connection.
$I < time\_stamp >< src\_addr >:< src\_port >< dst\_addr >:< dst\_port ><$
$n1 >< n2 >< n3 >< n4 >< n5 >$
The NAID module parses the interactivity message data stream and stores the information of the individual data fields.The NAID module then determines the smaller of the destination and source port numbers. This port is called the *server-port* and the host IP [5] address associated with the server-port is called the *server-host*. It assumes the server-host to be running a service on the server-port which is being accessed by a number of other hosts in the network. The NAID module then builds a string composed of server-host and server-port, *"server-host:server-port"*, called the *server-string*. The information of the individual data fields is added to the previous information stored for that server-string. For example, when the NAID module receives the following data stream, I 920986006.36404 132.235.17.1:3405 132.235.15.1:25 1.679000 162.625000 32.750000 0.003470 0.005993, it breaks the data stream and stores the individual fields. It determines the smaller of the two port numbers, 25, as the server-port and the host IP [5] address associated with the server-port, 132.235.15.1, as the server-host. It then builds the server-string "132.235.15.1:25". The information of the individual fields in the data stream is added to the previous information for server-string 132.235.15.1:25. Similarly all the interactivity messages about the currently open connections is used to build information for the respective server-strings.

After a profile time period, the module has information for every server-string that was involved in network activity. During this time period, the Total Interactivity of all the connections using a server-port on a particular server-host is obtained by adding the individual interactivity values of each connection to that server-port and server-host. The values of the Total ASOQ, Total ASOA, Total QAIT, Total AQIT are obtained in a similar manner. The Total NOC is obtained by counting the number of connection to that server port on the server host in that profile time period.

The operation of the intrusion detection using the ACSH approach is performed by the NAID module after every profile time period. The Total dimension values of all the connections for a server-string are obtained using the above described procedure. The average and standard deviation values for the server-string are obtained from the HDR. The Abnormality Factor (AF) for each dimension is obtained using the Abnormality Factor method described in Sect. 4. The sum of these Abnormality Factors is compared to a pre-defined threshold value to detect any abnormalities. When the sum of the Abnormality Factors is more than pre-defined threshold value an alert is generated. The alert indicates an abnormal activity in the server-host on that server-port during that profile time period. In case of an alert, the information of the individual connections causing the abnormality is stored in HDR. If the sum of the Abnormality Factors is less than pre-defined threshold value, it indicates normal behavior and the total dimension values are passed to the HDR, which calculates and stores the new average and standard deviation values for that server-string.

The process of comparision is done for all the server-strings involved in communication in the network for that profile time period. When the communication on a server-host and server-port takes place for the first time, the total dimension values are directly sent into the HDR. All the information built during the profile time period is cleared at the end of the comparisions and the process of detecting intrusions is repeated after every profile time period.

Currently, the NAID module does not maintain its own clock, but uses the time stamp from the open, close and network activity information received from the Current Data Repository. It receives information about network activity every 60 seconds. The NAID module periodically builds statistical profiles using the Abnormality Factor method for a profile time period of 60 seconds. At the end of each profile time period statistical comparisions are made to detect any intrusions.

5. Experiments and Results. The Information Systems Technology Group of MIT Lincoln Laboratory, under Defense Advanced Research Projects Agency (DARPA) Information Technology Office and Air Force Research Laboratory (AFRL/SNHS) sponsorship, has collected and distributed standard corpora for evaluation of computer network intrusion detection systems [8]. As a part of this evaluation plan, network traffic in the form of tcpdump files are collected on a simulation network and provided to the intrusion detection systems under test. This consists of one week of training data without any attacks to facilitate the training of anomaly detection systems and another week of test data with attack sessions containing recent attacks.

5.1. Experiment setup. Real-time Tcptrace reads and processes the tcpdump files. It generates open, close and interactivity messages, thereby simulating the real-time traffic captured in the tcpdump file. The data streams generated by the Real-time Tcptrace flow to the Current Data Repository. The NAID module registers with the Current Data Repository and requests the data streams reported by Real-time Tcptrace. The open, close, and interactiviy messages received from the Current Data Repository are analysed by the NAID module.

Initially, the first set of training data consisting of a week's data is run through the system to train the system to attain stable values of average and standard deviation. Later the second set of data consisting of attacks is run through the system to detect for any intrusions. The values of the parameters used during the tests are as follows:

- Real-time Tcptrace report time: 60 seconds
- NAID module profie time: 60 seconds
- Standardization Factor (SF): 3
- ACAH Threshold: 10
- ACSH Threshold: 10

The following sections provide the results obtained by running week 2 tuesday network dump file.

5.2. Results. The results obtained from the experiments are presented as graphs showing the variation of the current total w.r.t time for each dimension. The times shown on the graphs are relative, with the 0 representing the first time a connection was observed. Each of the graphs also show a standardization line, i.e. $Average + (StandardizationFactor * Std\_deviation)$ at every time instant. It is to be observed that all the current total values below the standardization line are considered normal and for all the other values, the abnormality factor is calculated for analysis. One of the graphs shows the variation of the total abnormality factor with time. This graph shows the times at which intrusion reports are generated by the NAID module.

5.2.1. ACAH approach of monitoring port 25(SMTP). The SMTP service running on Port 25 on all the hosts in the network is monitored in this approach. Figures 5.1 – 5.6 show the graphs for the 6 dimensions being monitored for port 25. Figure 5.7 shows the variation of total abnormality factor for all the dimensions with time. It can be seen that the total abnormality for this service is always below the threshold except for a peak between the time intervals 200 - 400 min. This peak clearly indicates abnormal behavior and is flagged as an attack by the NAID module.

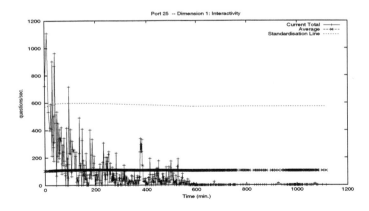

FIG. 5.1. *Port 25: Dimension Interactivity Vs Time*

5.2.2. ACSH appraoch of monitoring port 25 on host 172.6.112.50:. The SMTP service running on port 25 on the host 172.6.112.50 is monitored in this approach. Figures 5.8 – 5.13 show the graphs for the 6 dimensions being

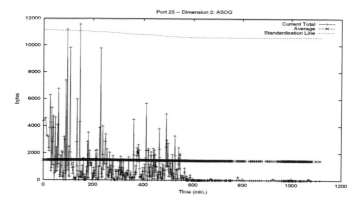

FIG. 5.2. *Port 25: Dimension ASOQ Vs Time*

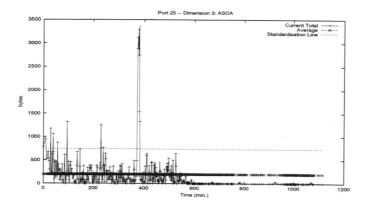

FIG. 5.3. *Port 25: Dimension ASOA Vs Time*

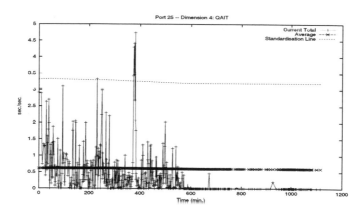

FIG. 5.4. *Port 25: Dimension QAIT Vs Time*

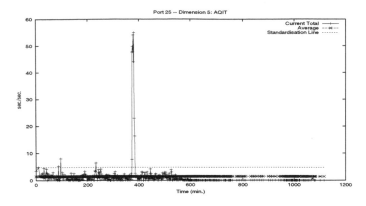

FIG. 5.5. *Port 25: Dimension AQIT Vs Time*

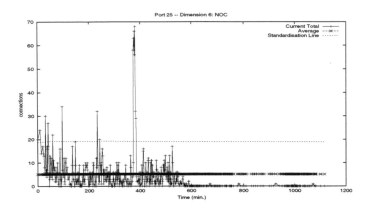

FIG. 5.6. *Port 25: Dimension NOC Vs Time*

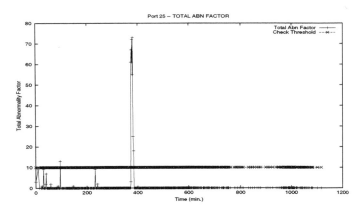

FIG. 5.7. *Port 25: Total Abnormality Factor Vs Time*

monitored for port 25 on host 172.6.112.50. Figure 5.14 shows the variation of total abnormality factor for all dimension with time. It can be clearly seen that this value is always below threshold except for a peak between the time intervals 300 - 400 min. This peak clearly indicates abnormal behavior and is flagged as an attack by the NAID module.

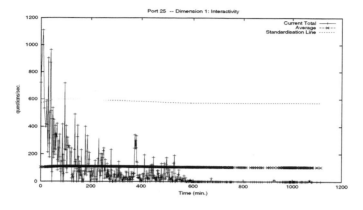

FIG. 5.8. *172.16.112.50:25: Dimension Interactivity Vs Time*

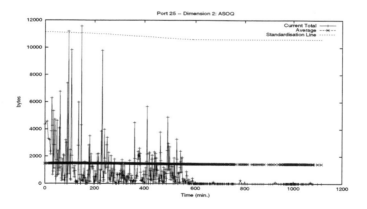

FIG. 5.9. *172.16.112.50:25: Dimension ASOQ Vs Time*

The intrusion attacks flagged in both the cases above are mail-bomb attacks which were carried on the simulated network. As it can be seen NAID module easily detects such an attack in real-time.

6. Conclusions and Future Work. The NAID module uses the data streams generated by Real-time Tcptrace to detect suspicious behavior of the network traffic. The use of Real-time Tcptrace is the major distinction between our approach and the approach taken by other intrusion detection systems. Real-time Tcptrace reports the data streams in real-time, thus enabling quicker and

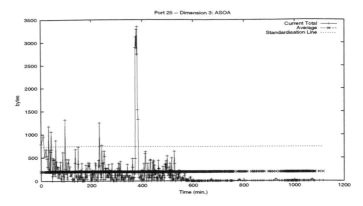

FIG. 5.10. *172.16.112.50:25: Dimension ASOA Vs Time*

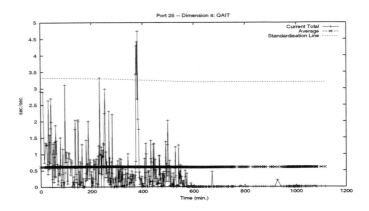

FIG. 5.11. *172.16.112.50:25: Dimension QAIT Vs Time*

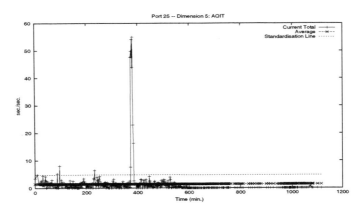

FIG. 5.12. *172.16.112.50:25: Dimension AQIT Vs Time*

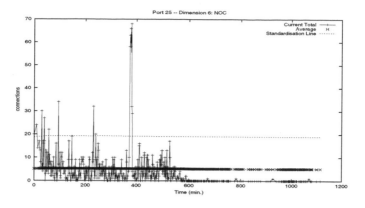

FIG. 5.13. *172.16.112.50:25: Dimension NOC Vs Time*

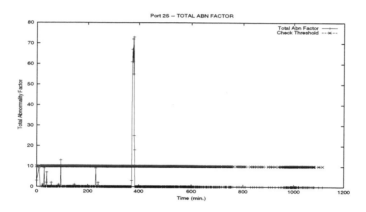

FIG. 5.14. *172.16.112.50:25: Total Abnormality Factor Vs Time*

real-time report of intrusion attacks. The NAID module detects intrusions depending on the behavior of the services running in the network. This approach
of behavioral monitoring enables NAID module to detect intrusions on various
services without any prior knowledge of the actual behavior of a service. The
use of the six dimensions: Interactivity, ASOQ, ASOA, QAIT, AQIT, and NOC
allows NAID module to profile the behavior of the serivces accurately. The two
approaches ACAH and ACSH have the capability of detecting some of the latest
e-mail viruses and also distributed attacks on a network.

The NAID module builds normal profile of a service during the process of
training its HDR. In the case of training in an actual network a certain number
of false positives are generated. Also, after the training process a certain number
of false positives are generated during its normal operation. Both these cases
may lead to under-calculation of the average and standard deviation values. As
a part of the future work, a new module is being developed which scans through

the intrusion alerts periodically and classifies the alerts as false positives or actual intrusions. It later sends the false positive alerts to HDR to be included for calculating the average and standard deviation values, thus maintaining a normal profile of a service.

The NAID module uses the Abnormality Factor method of statistical analysis, which may allow an intruder to generate a false negatives. An intruder can carry an attack over a long period of time by gradually increasing the average and standard deviation values over time and thus escaping any detection by the NAID module. Another aspect of the future work is concentrated on developing a more sensitive technique called Moving Average method. This technique maintains a moving average of the dimensions over a fixed window period which depicts the behavior of the dimensions in the last window. This particular moving average value is compared to the current value to determine any intrusion attacks.

The present system uses Real-time Tcptrace which currently reports the statistics of the connections established using TCP/IP [6]. This limits the intrusion capabilities of the NAID module and hence cannot detect intrusion attacks carried out using ICMP [13], UDP [12], etc. One of the future works is to extend the capability of Real-time Tcptrace to report statistics of connections established using other protocols.

The NAID module and its approaches presented in this paper are part of the first prototype of the INBOUNDS system which is undergoing a number of changes and developments to detect intrusions attacks more quickly and more efficiently.

REFERENCES

[1] D. Anderson, T. Frivold, and A. Valdes. Next-generation Intrusion Detection Expert System (NIDES). Technical Report SRI-CSL-95-07, SRI International, Computer Science Laboratory, SRI International, Menlo Park, CA 94025-3493, May 1995.

[2] S. Staniford Chen, S. Cheung, R. Crawford, M. Digler, J. Frank, J. Hoagland, K. Levitt, C. Lee, R. Yip, and D. Zerkle. GrIDS - A Graph Based Intrusion Detection System for Large Networks. In *19th National Information Systems Security Conference*, 1996.

[3] G.G. Cristoph, K.A. Jackson, M.C. Neumann, C. Siciliano, L.B. Ch, D.D. Simmonds, and C.A. Stallings. UNICORN: Misuse Detection for UNICOS. In *Proceedings of Supercomputing*, 1995.

[4] Dorothy E. Denning. An Intrusion-Detection Model. *IEEE Transactions on Software Engineering*, SE-13(2):222–232, February 1987.

[5] University of Southern California Information Sciences Institute. Internet Protocol. RFC 791, September 1981. http://www.ietf.org/rfc/rfc0791.txt.

[6] University of Southern California Information Sciences Institute. Transmission Control Protocol. RFC 793, September 1981. http://www.ietf.org/rfc/rfc0793.txt.

[7] Kathleen A. Jackson, David H. DuBois, and Cathy A. Stallings. An Expert System Application for Network Intrusion Detection. In *14th National Computer Security*

Conference, pages 215–225, Washington,D.C, OCtober 1991. National Institute of Standards and Technology/National Computer Security Center.

[8] MIT Lincoln Laboratory. DARPA Intrusion Detection Evaluation. http://www.ll.mit.edu/IST/ideval/.

[9] Teresa F. Lunt, R. Jagannathan, Rosanna Lee, Sherry Listgarten, David L. Edwards, Peter G. Neumann, Harold S. Javitz, and A. Valdes. IDES: The Enhanced Prototype, A Real-time Intrusion Detection System. Technical Report SRI Project 4185-010, SRI-CSL-88-12, CSL SRI International, Computer Science Laboratory, STI Intl. 333 Ravenswood Ave.,Menlo Park, CA 94925-3493, USA, October 1988.

[10] Shawn Osterman. Tcptrace. http://www.tcptrace.org/.

[11] Philip A. Porras and Peter G. Neumann. EMERALD: Event Monitoring Enabling Responses to Anomalous Live Disturbances. In *20th National Information Systems Security Conference*, pages 353–365, Baltimore, Maryland, USA, October 7-10 1997. National Institute of Standards and Technology/National Computer Security Center.

[12] J. Postel. User Datagram Protocol. RFC 768, August 1980. http://www.ietf.org/rfc/rfc0768.txt.

[13] J. Postel. Internet Control Message Protocol. RFC 792, September 1981. http://www.ietf.org/rfc/rfc0792.txt.

[14] Jonathan B. Postel. Simple Mail Transfer Protocol. RFC 821, August 1982. http://www.ietf.org/rfc/rfc0821.txt.

[15] P. Proctor. Audit Reduction and Misuse Detection in Heterogeneous Environments: Framework and Applications. In *Proceedings of the 15th National Computer Security Conference*, pages 117–125, December 1994.

[16] Michael M. Sebring, Eric Shellhouse, Mary E. Hanna, and R. Alan Whitehurst. Expert Systems in Intrusion Detection: A Case Study. In *Proceedings of the 11th National Computer Security Conference*, pages 74–81, Baltimore, Maryland, October 17-20 1988. National Institute of Standards and Technology.

[17] S.E. Smaha. Haystack: An Intrusion Detection System. In *IEEE Fourth Aerospace Computer Security Applications Conference*, IEEE Computer Society Press, December 1988. IEEE.

[18] S.E. Smaha and J. Winslow. Misuse Detection Tools. *Computer Security Journal*, 1994.

[19] Steven R. Snapp, Stephen E. Smaha, Daniel M. Teal, and Tim Grance. The DIDS (Distributed Intrusion Detection System) Prototype. In *Summer USENIX*, pages 227–233, San Antonio, Texas, June 8-12 1992. USENIX Association.

[20] Michael Sobirey. The Intrusion Detection System AID. http://www-rnks.informatik.tu-cottbus.de/ sobirey/aid.e.html.

[21] L.R. Welch, B.A. Shirazi, B. Ravindran, and C. Bruggeman. DeSiDeRaTa: QoS Management Technology for Dynamic, Scalable, Dependable, Real-Time Systems. In Proceedings of the 15th IFAC Workshop on Distributed Computer Control Systems, September 1998.

[22] G. White and V. Pooch. Cooperating Security Managers: Distributed Intrusion Detection Systems. *Computer & Security*, 15(5):441–450, 1996.

[23] J.R. Winkler and L.C. Landry. Intrusion and Anomaly detection, ISOA update. In *Proceedings of the 15th National Computer Security Conference*, pages 272–281, October 1992.

[24] Diego Zamboni, Jai S. Balasubramaniyan, Jose O. Garcia-Fernandez, David Isacoff, and Eugene Spafford. An Architecture for Intrusion Detection using Autonomous Agents. Technical Report 98/05, Purdue University, COAST Laboratory, Purdue University, West Lafayette, IN 47907-1398, June 1998.

ENERGY CONSUMPTION OF TRAFFIC PADDING SCHEMES IN WIRELESS AD HOC NETWORKS *

SHU JIANG AND NITIN H. VAIDYA AND WEI ZHAO †

Abstract. Wireless ad hoc network possesses some unique characteristics that prove to be extremely valuable in mission-critical systems. However, the wide use of wireless ad hoc network in mission-critical systems is still limited by its poor security and constraints on energy consumption – the nodes in wireless ad hoc networks typically have limited battery supply. It is well known that the wireless medium provides greater opportunities for eavesdropping on the transmissions of data packets in the network. While encryption may be used to hide message *contents* in the packets, the observable traffic *pattern* might reveal important information about the system. Traffic padding may be used to hide the traffic pattern, which means to insert dummy traffic into the network and present to the intruder a different traffic pattern. The apparent traffic pattern, which is observed by intruder, is referred to as a *cover mode* that hides the real operation mode of the system. Since the dummy traffic incurs an overhead, it is important to minimize dummy traffic while achieving the desired security objective. This paper deals with the issue of designing energy-saving traffic padding schemes. Instead of simply reducing the amount of dummy traffic, we attempt to develop cover modes that optimize system parameters, i.e. system lifetime and energy consumption per unit of real traffic delivered by the network.

Key words. traffic analysis, security scheme, traffic padding, wireless ad hoc network, energy consumption, performance evaluation

1. Introduction. Wireless ad hoc networks play an important role in mission-critical systems. The unique characteristics of wireless ad hoc network can facilitate such requirements in mission-critical systems as reliability, availability and maintainability in an efficient and economical way. Specifically, since a wireless ad hoc network can be formed by a group of computer nodes using peer-to-peer wireless links without making use of any pre-existing infrastructure [12], it is suitable for the mission-critical systems that require rapid deployment. The examples are battlefield communications and emergency operations such as fire and safety rescue operations. Another characteristic of wireless ad hoc network is its capability of self-configuration. A wireless ad hoc network is able to dynamically reconfigure its topology autonomously. The mission-critical systems can benefit from it in case of node failure or degradation of quality of service because new nodes can be deployed and operate instantly. However, the limitations of wireless ad hoc network should not be neglected, among which security and energy consumption may be the most critical ones. First, wireless ad hoc network is vulnerable to security attacks. In order to protect the data as well as the safety of operations in mission-critical system, various security measures can be taken. Second, wireless ad hoc network is energy-constrained.

---

*This research is sponsored by DARPA under contract number F30602-99-1-0531. Views and conclusions contained in this document are those of the authors and should not be interpreted as representing the official policies, either expressed or implied, of DARPA or the U.S. government.

†Department of Computer Science, Texas A&M University, College Station, TX 77843-3112, USA

Since any security measures inevitably consume system resources, their costs and influences on system performance must be evaluated properly. In most of the cases, a trade-off between security and performance must be made.

As in wired network, both active attacks and passive attacks are expected against a wireless ad hoc network [23]. Active attacks involve modification of the data packets flowing in the network or creation of fake data. The goal of the intruder is to disrupt the network service and bring the whole system down. Passive attacks are in the nature of eavesdropping on, or monitoring of, transmissions. The goal of the intruder is to obtain information. It is well known that the wireless medium provides greater opportunities for eavesdropping, as compared to a wired network. Many approaches can be used to combat this problem – one class of techniques makes it difficult to eavesdrop on wireless transmissions (e.g., frequency-hopping using a secret hopping pattern), and another class of techniques makes it difficult to learn useful information even if an eavesdropper can hear the wireless transmissions. This paper is related to the latter approach.

When an intruder can hear wireless transmissions, two types of information may potentially be obtained:

- Contents of the transmitted packets: To prevent an intruder from learning the contents, the transmitted packets can be encrypted. This paper assumes that such an encryption mechanism is being used.
- Traffic pattern: Even with encryption, an intruder can potentially learn useful information by observing the traffic pattern or changes of traffic pattern. For example, in a military network, a significant change of traffic pattern may imply impending action, change of capabilities, change of chains of command or change of level of readiness [6]. This type of security attack is referred to as the *traffic analysis*[23].

Previous studies show that a technique called *traffic padding* can be used to protect the traffic pattern information in combination with data encryption method [1, 19]. The idea is simple. In addition to real data packets, the network also transmits some dummy packets. A dummy packet has authentic header but a dummy message in payload. Just from packet header, which carries address information, the dummy packet is not differentiable from a real packet. In order to fool an eavesdropper in believing that a dummy packet is real, the packet payload is encrypted with a secret key shared between source node and destination node of the packet.

The major concern on traffic padding is its performance. Dummy packets allow a lightly loaded flow to have its apparent load increased at the cost of additional traffic in the network. Processing dummy packets consumes the premium network resources and might degrade the quality of service received by real data packets. In previous work done in our group, we addressed this problem in the context of real-time network [11, 9, 10]. We proposed and analyzed methods that efficiently hide the network traffic pattern and still satisfy the worst-case delay constraints on user data packets in an internetwork. Our scheme utilized both traffic padding and traffic rerouting techniques and has been implemented in a testbed network [10].

In this paper, we will study the energy consumption performance of different traffic padding schemes in the context of wireless ad hoc network. We consider the situation wherein the network may operate in any one of many possible *operation modes* (each operation mode has a distinct traffic pattern). A *cover mode* is constructed such that the intruder cannot determine the real operation mode of the network at any given time. In addition, to make it difficult to detect the change of operation mode, our schemes use an identical cover mode for all operation modes. We propose several schemes for constructing such a cover mode and evaluate their performance. Specifically, as elaborated later, we consider *end-to-end* as well as *link-level* approaches for padding traffic.

Insertion of padding traffic in the network leads to higher energy consumption. We consider two metrics to characterize energy consumption with and without traffic padding: the first metric measures the system lifetime, and the second metric is the amount of energy consumption for delivering a unit of user data. These metrics are explained later in the paper.

The rest of the paper is organized as follows. Section II presents our network model and discusses the two schemes of constructing cover mode. In Section III, we give the formal definition of performance metrics and formulate the problem of deriving individual metrics as different optimal routing problems. Heuristic solutions to those problems are provided in Section IV. Section V presents our simulations results of comparing the performance of different cover modes. Finally, Section VI concludes the paper and discusses the future work.

2. Preliminaries. For the purpose of this paper, we will assume that there are n nodes in the network; the network is completely connected; and the network operates in one of M different operation modes, which correspond to different known states of the system. Two modes differ either in the sets of traffic flows that are active in the network, or in the traffic demands posed by the flows, or both. The set of traffic flows and their respective traffic demands define a traffic pattern in the network in a particular mode. For simplicity, we use the average traffic rate of a flow to represent its traffic demand in this paper.

There are two types of traffic flows: end-to-end flow and link flow. Both are data packet streams flowing in the network but are different in many aspects. The source and destination of an end-to-end flow might be any pair of nodes in the network, while link flows only exist between neighboring nodes. For end-to-end flow, if its source node and destination node are not adjacent with each other, the flow traffic traverses a multi-hop route which contains a set of intermediate nodes as well as "links" between neighboring nodes. Note that link in a wireless network has only logical sense. Physically, all transmissions from a node to its neighbors share the same wireless channel. For the ease of discussion, we say that packets from node X to its neighbor Y traverse "link" (X,Y). A link flow on link (X,Y) is the aggregate of all end-to-end flows whose routes include link (X,Y). Thus, the average rate of a link flow is the sum of the rates of all relevant end-to-end flows.

Traffic matrix is often used to describe traffic patterns. In a traffic matrix $R = (r_{ij})_{n \times n}$ that represents an end-to-end flow traffic pattern, r_{ij} is the average rate of the flow from node i to j. If $r_{ij} = 0$, it means that there is no traffic from node i to j in this particular mode. When $R = (r_{ij})_{n \times n}$ represents a link flow traffic pattern, r_{ij} is equal to zero for all pairs of non-adjacent nodes.

In terms of threat model, we consider intruders who are able to eavesdrop all transmissions in the network. Even though it is more likely that only some links in the network are under surveillance, those intruders are still extremely difficult to locate due to the broadcast characteristic of wireless medium. So in this paper, the design of security system is based on the assumption that the intruders might appear anywhere in the network at any time. The goal of the intruder is to determine the system operation mode from the observed traffic pattern, while the goal of the system is to prevent the release of this information. The system achieves this goal by presenting to the intruder a stable and time-invariant traffic pattern which defines a *cover mode* of the network.

Depending on the type of target traffic pattern, we can define *end-to-end cover mode*, which maintains constant traffic rate of each end-to-end flow, or *link cover mode*, which maintains constant traffic rate on each link. End-to-end cover mode and link cover mode are implemented by different traffic padding schemes. In the following, we describe the two traffic padding schemes and give a qualitative comparison between them. In the next section, we define new metrics for measuring the performance of cover mode regarding energy consumption.

2.1. End-to-end Traffic Padding Scheme. Consider two operation modes, with traffic rate r_{ij}^1 and r_{ij}^2, respectively, for the flow from node i to node j. To keep the traffic rate from i to j constant regardless of the operation mode, the end-to-end flow must reserve a bandwidth of at least $\max(r_{ij}^1, r_{ij}^2)$. Without loss of generality, let us assume that $r_{ij}^1 \leq r_{ij}^2$. When the network is operating in the first operation mode, dummy packets (i.e., padding traffic) must be generated at node i at the rate of $r_{ij}^2 - r_{ij}^1$ to maintain an apparent traffic rate of $\max(r_{ij}^1, r_{ij}^2)$, which is equal to r_{ij}^2. These packets traverse the entire route taken by the flow. The flow destination identifies the dummy packets and discards them on receipt. The rate at which dummy packets are inserted is independent of the *route*.

Also, intermediate nodes on the flow's route need not take any special actions to implement the cover mode. Assuming that all transmitted packets of a flow are encrypted and decrypted at the source and destination node respectively, using a key not disclosed to any third party, i.e. end-to-end encryption, even if the intruders compromise all intermediate nodes on the route, they are not able to acquire the message contents encapsulated in the packets.

For future reference, remember that packets belonging to a given flow always traverse the same route. Thus, when an end-to-end cover mode is implemented, in addition to the end-to-end flows maintaining constant traffic rates, the link flow traffic rate for each link in the ad hoc network also remains constant, independent of the operation mode, as long as the network topology is fixed and the routes taken by all the flows are not changed.

2.2. Link Traffic Padding Scheme. The link traffic padding scheme implements a link cover mode by inserting dummy packets on per-link basis so as to maintain constant traffic rate on each link, independent of the actual operation mode. That is, for link (X,Y), node X needs to generate and send dummy packets, and node Y must identify and remove the dummy packets received on link (X,Y). (Recall that when using the end-to-end cover mode, only the destination node of an end-to-end flow has to be able to identify the dummy packets.) The dummy packets may be made to belong to any end-to-end flow carried on this link.

Like in end to end cover mode, the apparent traffic rate of a link flow should be equal to or greater than the maximal possible rate of traffic on this link over all operation modes. As mentioned, the traffic rate of a link flow is the sum of traffic rates of all end-to-end flows that traverse the link. Therefore, it is not only decided by the end-to-end flow traffic patterns but also the routes taken by all the flows. This is unlike the end-to-end cover mode (which can be determined independent of the chosen routes). On the other hand, although the link traffic rate on each link is constant in the link cover mode (independent of the real operation mode), the end-to-end flows passing through the link may present different rates in different operation modes. Thus, a link encryption mechanism is expected in use so that: (a) the link receiver can distinguish dummy packets from the real packets, but an eavesdropper cannot, and (b) an eavesdropper cannot determine the end-to-end (source, destination) for a given packet.

As observed above, an end-to-end cover mode also yields constant link traffic rates – thus, an end-to-end cover mode is also a link cover mode (however, the converse is not always true). In general, a link cover mode can be implemented by inserting a smaller amount of dummy traffic, as compared to implementing an end-to-end cover mode. An intuitive explanation is that each dummy packet traverses only one link in a link cover mode, whereas each dummy packet traverses the entire route in an end-to-end cover mode. The advantage of this per-link traffic padding is that each link has control on the amount of padding traffic and inserts only the necessary amount of it. The disadvantage is at the extra cost of link encryption and the processing cost of dummy packets at each node. Thus, both approaches have their advantages and disadvantages.

We now illustrate the difference between end-to-end and link cover modes using an example.

Example: Consider the network of 3 nodes, illustrated in Fig. 2.1 and 2.2. Assume that this network has two operation modes. Mode 1 consists of one flow from node A to C at the rate of 4 data units/sec, and another flow from B to C at the rate of 7 data units/sec. Mode 2 consists of a flow from node A to B at the rate of 1 data unit/sec and a flow from node B to C at the rate of 10 data units/sec. Fig. 2.1(a) shows the two operation modes.

From the prior discussion, it follows that an *end-to-end cover mode* contain-

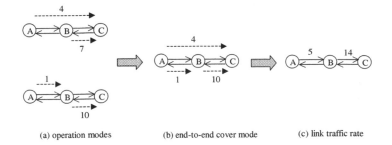

(a) operation modes   (b) end-to-end cover mode   (c) link traffic rate

FIG. 2.1. *Produce end-to-end cover mode*

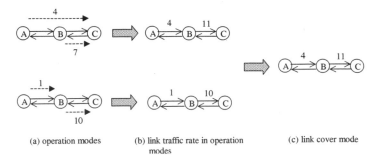

(a) operation modes   (b) link traffic rate in operation   (c) link cover mode
                                  modes

FIG. 2.2. *Produce link cover mode*

ing three flows can be obtained as follows: (i) a flow from A to B at 1 data unit/sec, (ii)a flow from A and C at 4 data units/sec, and (iii) a flow from B and C at 10 data units/sec. The end-to-end cover mode is illustrated in Fig. 2.1(b). Fig. 2.1(c) illustrates the link traffic rates obtained for this end-to-end cover mode, taking into account the routes taken by the flows. Observe that there is traffic with rate 5 data units/sec on link (A, B) and with rate 14 data units/sec on link (B, C).

Now, Fig. 2.2 illustrates a link cover mode for the same two operation modes, which are also shown in Fig. 2.2(a). To obtain the link cover mode, we first determine the link traffic rate for each of the operation modes, taking into account the routes used by these flows. The link traffic rates for the two modes are shown in Fig. 2.2(b). Fig. 2.2(c) illustrates the *link cover mode* for this example – link traffic rate for a link, say (X,Y), in this link cover mode is obtained as the maximum link traffic rate on the link over all operation modes. For instance, traffic rate on link (A, B) is 4 data units/sec in mode 1 and 1 data unit/sec in mode 2. Thus, in the link cover mode, the link traffic rate is $\max(4, 1) = 4$ (data units/sec).

Comparing Fig. 2.1(c) and Fig. 2.2(c), observe that, the link cover mode has a lower bandwidth requirements than the end-to-end cover mode.

3. The Performance Model. In general, when using either of the two traffic padding schemes above, the produced cover mode introduces additional traffic in the network which consumes additional energy. Since energy resource is often restricted in wireless hosts, utility of a security scheme depends on the extent to which it affects the energy requirements. We define two performance metrics to evaluate the impact of cover mode upon system operations, which are *system lifetime* and *energy consumption per unit of real data* respectively.

The network is represented by a directed graph $G(N, L)$ where N is the set of all nodes and L is a set of directed links. Link (i, j) is in L (where $i, j \in N$) if node j can receive packets from node i directly. Define a set S_i for each node i, such that node $j \in S_i$ if and only if $(i, j) \in L$, i.e., S_i is the set of nodes within node i's transmitter range. We also define the following notations:

W a set of end-to-end flows

r_w average traffic rate of an end-to-end flow w

P_w set of all candidate routes for an end-to-end flow w.

$x_{p,w}$ routing decision variable which is 1 if path p is used for end-to-end flow w and 0 otherwise.

$\delta_{ij}(p)$ indicator function which is 1 if link (i, j) is on path p and 0 otherwise.

λ_{ij} traffic rate on link $(i, j) \in L$

E_i initial energy level at node $i \in N$

τ energy consumed when a node transmits unit data

ρ energy consumed when a node receives unit data

e_i rate of energy consumption at node $i \in N$

W and r_w for each end-to-end flow w in W specify an end-to-end flow traffic pattern, i.e. operation mode. For one end-to-end flow, P_w, $x_{p,w}$ and $\delta_{ij}(p)$ fully defines the route taken by the flow. For the purpose of this paper, we assume that all packets belonging to an end-to-end flow are routed along the same route. This type of routing is provided, for instance, by the Dynamic Source Routing (DSR) protocol [15] for ad hoc networks. We do not consider multi-path routing that allows the packets from the same flow be routed along multiple routes, due to the potential difficulties created by reordering of packets. Given an end-to-end flow traffic pattern, different routes taken by the flows produce different link flow traffic patterns because the traffic rate on a link is the sum of the traffic rates of all end-to-end flows carried by that link. The relationship between these system variables are stated in the following equations.

$$(3.1) \qquad\qquad\qquad \sum_{p \in P_w} x_{p,w} = 1$$

$$(3.2) \qquad\qquad\qquad \lambda_{ij} = \sum_{p,w:p \in P_w, w \in W} x_{p,w} r_w \delta_{ij}(p)$$

At each node, energy is consumed when the node is transmitting or receiving data packets. The energy consumption rate depends on the rates at which packets are arriving and leaving, i.e link flow traffic rates. But, the energy required for transmitting same amount of data is typically much higher than that for receiving. For instance, the DEC Roamabout radio consumes approximately 5.76 watts during transmission and 2.88 watts during receiving [22]. A 915MHz Lucent WaveLAN PCMCIA wireless Ethernet card requires 3.00 watts when transmitting and 1.48 watts when receiving [16]. This fact is stated in the following equation:

$$(3.3) \qquad e_i = \tau \sum_{j \in S_i} \lambda_{ij} + \rho \sum_{j:i \in S_j} \lambda_{ji}$$

In the rest of the paper, when we identify parameters that relate to a particular mode, superscript (m), EC, LC are added to the notation representing mode m, end-to-end cover mode, link cover mode respectively. For example, $W^{(1)}$ denotes the set of end-to-end flows in mode 1 and λ_{ij}^{LC} denotes the traffic rate on link (i, j) in a link cover mode.

3.1. System Lifetime T_{sys}. The system lifetime is defined as the duration of time which elapses before at least one node is depleted of energy. Assuming that the energy reserve at each node is not recoverable, it declines at the energy consumption rate until it reaches zero level.[1] When either end-to-end cover mode or link cover mode is implemented, the link flow traffic pattern is constant regardless of the real operation mode, which means that e_i, the energy consumption rate at node i, is constant as well. We are able to give the formulas for calculating T_{sys} in either cover mode as below.

$$(3.4) \qquad T_{sys}^{EC} = \min_{i \in N} \frac{E_i}{e_i^{EC}}$$

$$(3.5) \qquad = \min_{i \in N} \frac{E_i}{\tau \sum_{j \in S_i} \lambda_{ij}^{EC} + \rho \sum_{j:i \in S_j} \lambda_{ji}^{EC}}$$

and

$$(3.6) \qquad T_{sys}^{LC} = \min_{i \in N} \frac{E_i}{e_i^{LC}}$$

$$(3.7) \qquad = \min_{i \in N} \frac{E_i}{\tau \sum_{j \in S_i} \lambda_{ij}^{LC} + \rho \sum_{j:i \in S_j} \lambda_{ji}^{LC}}$$

Observe that T_{sys}^{EC} is a function of the link flow traffic pattern in the end-to-end cover mode. When all operation modes are given, the rate of each flow in the end-to-end cover mode may be obtained simply as a maximum rate of this flow over all modes - it is easy to see that any cover mode that uses flow traffic rates

---

[1]It was observed that the battery recovers its capacity slowly when no data is sent [4]. Therefore, the burstiness of traffic can be utilized (or regulated) to extend the battery life. However, we assume a simple, linear battery lifetime declination model in this paper.

higher than this will necessarily result in higher energy consumption and shorter system lifetime. (Note that if flow w is not active in a certain operation mode, its rate is essentially 0 in that mode.) Then the system lifetime in the end-to-end cover mode solely depends on the routes taken by all the flows. We choose the optimal routes so that the system lifetime is maximized over all possible routing plans. This optimal routing problem can be formulated as follows:

$$(3.1) \qquad\qquad Maximize \quad T_{sys}^{EC}$$

subject to:

$$(8) \qquad T_{sys}^{EC} * (\tau \sum_{j \in S_i} \lambda_{ij}^{EC} + \rho \sum_{j:i \in S_j} \lambda_{ji}^{EC}) \leq E_i, \quad \forall i \in N$$

$$(9) \qquad \lambda_{ij}^{EC} = \sum_{p,w:p \in P_w, w \in W^{EC}} x_{p,w} r_w \delta_{ij}(p), \quad \forall (i,j) \in L$$

$$(10) \qquad \sum_{p \in P_w} x_{p,w} = 1, \quad \forall w \in W^{EC}$$

and

$$(11) \qquad x_{p,w} = 0 \ or \ 1, \quad \forall p \in P_w \ \forall w \in W^{EC}$$

where W^{EC} is the set of end-to-end flows in the end-to-end cover mode.

This problem turns out to be a 0-1 integer linear programming problem, which is NP-complete [7]. There are no polynomial algorithms for solving this problem optimally. In Section IV, we present a heuristic algorithm based on the flow deviation (FD) method [17, 2] to find a locally optimal solution.

The reasoning above applies to T_{sys}^{LC} too. However, in a link cover mode, there is not a constant set of end-to-end flows. The traffic rate on each link is the maximal possible rate of real traffic on that link in any operation mode. Formally, if there are M operation modes in the network, the traffic rate on link (i, j) in the link cover mode is given by

$$(12) \qquad \lambda_{ij}^{LC} = \max_m(\lambda_{ij}^{(m)}), \quad m = 1, 2, \ldots, M$$

where $\lambda_{ij}^{(m)}$ depends on the routes taken by end-to-end flows in mode m. We are about to find the optimal route for each end-to-end flow in each mode so that the resultant link cover mode produces the maximal system lifetime. The optimal routing problem can be stated as follows:

(3.2) $$Maximize \quad T_{sys}^{LC}$$

subject to:

(13) $$T_{sys}^{LC} * (\tau \sum_{j \in S_i} \lambda_{ij}^{LC} + \rho \sum_{j:i \in S_j} \lambda_{ji}^{LC}) \le E_i, \quad \forall i \in N$$

(14) $$\lambda_{ij}^{LC} = \max_m(\lambda_{ij}^{(m)}), \quad m = 1, 2, \ldots, M$$

(15) $$\lambda_{ij}^{(m)} = \sum_{p,w:p \in P_w, w \in W^{(m)}} x_{p,w} r_w \delta_{ij}(p), \quad \forall(i,j) \in L \ \forall m$$

(16) $$\sum_{p \in P_w} x_{p,w} = 1, \quad \forall w \in W^{(m)} \ \forall m$$

and

(17) $$x_{p,w} = 0 \ or \ 1, \quad \forall p \in P_w \ \forall w \in W^{(m)} \ \forall m$$

where $W^{(m)}$ is the set of end-to-end flows in mode m.

This problem is a 0-1 integer linear programming problem with nonlinear constraints. Thus it is difficult to solve optimally. Again, we take the flow deviation method. A heuristic algorithm is proposed in next section.

For the purpose of comparison, we intend to find the system lifetime when no traffic padding scheme is activated. Unlike in end-to-end cover mode or link cover mode, the link traffic rates change as the system switches its operation mode. A direct implication of this instability of link traffic pattern is that the energy consumption rate at each node does not remain constant. In other words, a node loses its energy reserve in a non-linear fashion. Instead of pursuing the exact value of system lifetime, we take a different approach. We derive the would-be system lifetime if the system were to stay in each particular operation mode all the time (assuming optimal routing of end-to-end flows so as to maximize the system lifetime). Among the M results we obtain, the lowest value and the highest value must be the lower bound and upper bound on actual system lifetime, respectively. A formal proof is not provided here due to the space limit. However, this property is illustrated in Fig. 3.1 using a two operation mode system as example. In the figure, $T_i^{(m)}$ is the would-be lifetime of node i if system were to be in mode m and never change. In reality, system switches operation mode back and force. Thus, the energy consumption rate at a node changes over the time (as reflected by the curve in the figure).

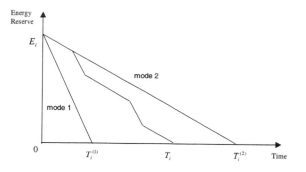

FIG. 3.1. *The non-linear energy consumption rate at node i*

It worths mentioning that our definition of system lifetime is similar to the one presented in [3]. However, while our definition attempts to take into account both energy consumption when transmitting a packet as well as when receiving a packet, [3] only considers energy consumption when transmitting packets. So our definition is somewhat more accurate than [3] – nevertheless, our definition (similar to [3]) ignores the power consumed by nodes when they overhear transmissions not intended for them. Our energy consumption model is more accurately applicable for power-conserving MAC protocols such as PAMAS [22], which turn off radios when not actively needed to receive or transmit a packet.

3.2. Energy Consumption Per Unit Real Data $\bar{e}$. The metric $\bar{e}$ is designed to measure the unit cost of delivering user data in terms of energy consumption. It is calculated as the total amount of energy consumed at all nodes (for transmitting and receiving both real data packets and dummy packets) divided by the amount of real data delivered within the unit time period. Since the network throughput of real data changes as the network changes its operation mode, the value of $\bar{e}$ at any given time depends on not only the link traffic pattern of the cover mode, which the network is in, but also the real operation mode, which is hidden. We use notations $\bar{e}^{EC}(m)$ and $\bar{e}^{LC}(m)$ to denote the energy consumption per unit real data in end-to-end cover mode and in link cover mode, respectively, while network is in operation mode m. According to their definitions, $\bar{e}^{EC}(m)$ and $\bar{e}^{LC}(m)$ are calculated as

$$(18) \qquad \bar{e}^{EC}(m) = \frac{\sum_{i \in N} e_i^{EC}}{\sum_{w \in W^{(m)}} r_w}$$

$$(19) \qquad = \frac{\sum_{i \in N} (\tau \sum_{j \in S_i} \lambda_{ij}^{EC} + \rho \sum_{j:i \in S_j} \lambda_{ji}^{EC})}{\sum_{w \in W^{(m)}} r_w}$$

and

$$(20) \qquad \bar{e}^{LC}(m) = \frac{\sum_{i \in N} e_i^{LC}}{\sum_{w \in W^{(m)}} r_w}$$

$$(21) \qquad = \frac{\sum_{i \in N}(\tau \sum_{j \in S_i} \lambda_{ij}^{LC} + \rho \sum_{j:i \in S_j} \lambda_{ji}^{LC})}{\sum_{w \in W^{(m)}} r_w}$$

Like T_{sys}^{EC}, $\bar{e}^{EC}(m)$ is a function of the link flow traffic pattern in the end-to-end cover mode. Since the set of end-to-end flows and their respective rates are already determined, its value solely depends on the routes taken by the flows. We choose the optimal routes so that $\bar{e}^{EC}(m)$ is minimized over all possible routing plans. From Equation (19), it follows that minimizing $\bar{e}^{EC}(m)$ is equivalent to minimizing the aggregate energy consumption rate of the network, which is the nominator of the fraction. Observe that, if an end-to-end flow w has rate r_w, then, *at each hop* on its path, the transmission of the packets contributes energy consumption at the rate $(\tau + \rho) * r_w$ (this includes energy consumed at transmitting and receiving endpoints of the link). Therefore, the route with the minimal number of hops, i.e. the shortest hop route, is the optimal route for w. This property can be extended to the case when no cover mode is being used. In order to minimize the energy consumption per unit data delivered, all end-to-end flows must be routed along their respective shortest hop routes.

The problem of minimizing $\bar{e}^{LC}(m)$ through optimal routing is much harder than its counterpart with respect to end-to-end cover mode. In the link cover mode, the aggregate energy consumption rate of the network is

$$(22) \qquad \sum_{i \in N}(\tau \sum_{j \in S_i} \lambda_{ij}^{LC} + \rho \sum_{j:i \in S_j} \lambda_{ji}^{LC})$$

where λ_{ij}^{LC} is given by Equation (12). The problem of minimizing the aggregate energy consumption rate is another integer programming problem and is as hard as problem 3.2 (see below).

$$(3.3) \qquad Minimize \quad \sum_{i \in N}(\tau \sum_{j \in S_i} \lambda_{ij}^{LC} + \rho \sum_{j:i \in S_j} \lambda_{ji}^{LC})$$

subject to:

$$(23) \qquad \lambda_{ij}^{LC} = \max_m(\lambda_{ij}^{(m)}), \quad m = 1, 2, \ldots, M$$

$$(24) \qquad \lambda_{ij}^{(m)} = \sum_{p,w:p \in P_w, w \in W^{(m)}} x_{p,w} r_w \delta_{ij}(p), \quad \forall (i,j) \in L \; \forall m$$

$$(25) \qquad \sum_{p \in P_w} x_{p,w} = 1, \quad \forall w \in W^{(m)} \; \forall m$$

and

$$(26) \qquad x_{p,w} = 0 \; or \; 1, \quad \forall p \in P_w \; \forall w \in W^{(m)} \; \forall m$$

where $W^{(m)}$ is the set of end-to-end flows in mode m.

4. Routing Algorithm. In this section, we try to solve the optimal routing problems defined in Section III. Our solution is a heuristic routing algorithm based on flow deviation method[17, 2]. First, we briefly describe the flow deviation method. Then we show how this method can be used to cope with those problems individually.

4.1. Flow deviation method [17, 2]. Flow deviation (FD) method is a general method for solving nonlinear programming problems. A FD-based algorithm is divided into two phases: the *initialization* phase and the *updating* phase. In the initialization phase, an initial solution of the problem is found. In our case, to form the initial solution, we choose a shortest hop path for each end-to-end flow. Then the FD algorithm enters *updating* phase in which the initial solution is improved incrementally by changing the routing paths of some end-to-end flows. The rerouting of end-to-end flows is not made simultaneously; instead, one end-to-end flow is selected at one time whose path is established with the goal to optimize the objective function. Through coordinated rerouting process, a locally optimal routing solution can be reached ultimately.

FD-based Routing Algorithm.

(1) Compute the shortest hop path for each end-to-end flow.
(2) Select an end-to-end flow w randomly or according to a sequence defined in advance. If the sequence is exhausted, it is simply repeated.
(3) Remove the traffic requirement r_w for w from the network.
(4) Fix the routing paths for all other end-to-end flows and reroute the selected end-to-end flow w aiming to optimize the objective function.
(5) If rerouting of flow w does not improve the objective function, restore its old routing path.
(6) Go to step (2) until all the end-to-end flows have been examined once, but no further improvements are possible.

In the worst case, the algorithm takes exponential time to converge. But it can be efficient in a probabilistic sense. [25] proves that the algorithm takes $O(n^2)$ iterations on average where $n = |N|$ is the number of nodes in the network.

4.2. Solution for problem 3.1. The objective function in this problem is T_{sys}^{EC}, the system lifetime in an end-to-end cover mode. In the FD-based routing algorithm, the rerouting of the selected end-to-end flow w, whose source is node s and destination is node d, intends to find the optimal path maximizing the objective function. For a given path p from node s to node d, the would-be system lifetime (denoted by T'_{sys}) – that is the system lifetime if path p were to be chosen to send packets from s to d – is

$$(1) \quad T'_{sys} = \min(\frac{E_s}{e_{s,w} + \tau r_w}, \frac{E_d}{e_{d,w} + \rho r_w}, \min_{k \in N_p, k \neq s, k \neq d} \frac{E_k}{c_{k,w} + (\tau + \rho)r_w})$$

where N_p is the set of all nodes on path p and $e_{k,w}$ is the energy consumption rate by node k excluding any energy consumption by flow w.

Finding a path maximizing T'_{sys} is equivalent to finding a path minimizing the following value:

$$(2) \qquad \max\left(\frac{e_{s,w} + \tau r_w}{E_s}, \frac{e_{d,w} + \rho r_w}{E_d}, \max_{k \in N_p, k \neq s, k \neq d} \frac{e_{k,w} + (\tau + \rho)r_w}{E_k}\right)$$

because E_s, E_d and E_k all are constants here. If we define the weight of a path as in (2), then the path for w is the one with the minimal weight value. Bellman-Ford algorithm [5] can be used here to find the path. In the algorithm, when we check a new path from source node s to node i which is constructed by concatenating a known path from s to node j with link (j, i), the weight of the new path $p_{sj} + (j, i)$ is calculated by the following formula:

$$(3) \qquad \max\left(Weight(p_{sj}), \frac{e_{j,w} + (\tau + \rho)r_w}{E_j}, \frac{e_{i,w} + \rho r_w}{E_i}\right)$$

The pseudo code of the algorithm is given below.

Bellman-Ford Algorithm.

(1) for each node $i \in N$
        $Weight(p_{si}) = 0$.
(2) for $k = 1$ to $|N| - 1$
        for each link $(j, i) \in L$
          if $Weight(p_{sj} + (j, i)) < Weight(p_{si})$,
        then
            replace p_{si} with path $p_{sj} + (j, i)$.
(3) return p_{sd}.

Step (1) initializes the variables. Step (2) performs the relax operation. After k-th iteration, the weighted shortest path from source node s to each node with no more than k hops is found. Since there are no negatively weighted links, the algorithm will converge to a path that satisfies our needs after $|N| - 1$ iterations.

4.3. Solution for the problem 3.2. The objective function in this problem is T^{LC}_{sys}, the system lifetime in a link cover mode. According to Equation (3.7), routing decision must be made for each end-to-end flow in each operation mode, and same flow may end up with taking different routes in different operation modes. When using FD-based routing algorithm to find a routing solution, we immediately face the problem: "which end-to-end flow in which mode should be picked up?". A two-level approach is taken here. We select one mode at one time and improve the routing paths for the end-to-end flows in that mode while the routing paths for flows in all other modes are fixed. Then we switch to another mode and repeat the intra-mode improvement process. If all modes have been selected once and no improvements can be made, the algorithm stops.

During the intra-mode optimization, the FD-based algorithm in Section IV(A) is used with one end-to-end flow being selected at one time. The rerouting of the selected end-to-end flow w intends to find the optimal path that maximizes the objective function. Without loss of generality, w is assumed to be one of the end-to-end flows in mode 1, whose source is node s and destination is node d. Let $\bar{\lambda}_{ij}^{(1)}$ be the rate of real traffic on link $(i,j) \in L$ in mode 1 with the removal of r_w. Let $e_{k,w}$ be the energy consumption rate by node k in the cover mode after flow w being removed. If link (i,j) were to be on the path for w, then the traffic rate on (i,j) in the link cover mode would increase by

$$(4) \quad \Delta\lambda_{ij}^{LC} = \max_{m}(\bar{\lambda}_{ij}^{(1)} + r_w, \lambda_{ij}^{(2)}, \dots, \lambda_{ij}^{(m)}) - \max_{m}(\bar{\lambda}_{ij}^{(1)}, \lambda_{ij}^{(2)}, \dots, \lambda_{ij}^{(m)})$$

If a given path p from node s to node d were to be used, the system lifetime would be

$$T'_{sys} = \min_{k \in N_p} \frac{E_k}{e_{k,w} + \tau \sum_{j \in S_k} \Delta\lambda_{kj}^{LC}\delta_{kj}(p) + \rho \sum_{i:k \in S_i} \Delta\lambda_{ik}^{LC}\delta_{ik}(p)}$$

where N_p is the set of all nodes on path p. The problem of maximizing T'_{sys} has a dual problem of minimizing the following value:

$$(5) \quad \max_{k \in N_p} \frac{e_{k,w} + \tau \sum_{j \in S_k} \Delta\lambda_{kj}^{LC}\delta_{kj}(p) + \rho \sum_{i:k \in S_i} \Delta\lambda_{ik}^{LC}\delta_{ik}(p)}{E_k}$$

So, if we assign each link $(i,j) \in L$ with weight $\Delta\lambda_{ij}^{LC}$ and define the weight of a path as in (5), then the optimal path for w is the one with the minimal weight value.

We propose the following extended Bellman-Ford (EBF) algorithm to find the path. In the original Bellman-Ford algorithm, at its k-th iteration, it identifies the optimal (in our context: minimal weight) path between the source node s and each node i, containing no more than k hops. EBF extends the Bellman-Ford algorithm by having each node i maintain a set of paths, $PATH(i)$. $PATH(i)$ records the optimal path from s to i through each input link of i. For instance, if $(v,i) \in L$, then the optimal path from s to i through (v,i) is recorded in $PATH(i)$ as $p_{si}(v)$, i.e., $PATH(i) = \{p_{si}(v)|i \in S_v\}$. During the relax operation, when we check a new path from source node s to node i which is constructed by concatenating a known path from s to node j in $PATH(j)$, $p_{sj}(u)$, with link (j,i), the weight of the new path $p_{sj}(u) + (j,i)$ is calculated by the following formula:

$$(6) \quad \max(Weight(p_{sj}(u)), \frac{e_{j,w} + \tau\Delta\lambda_{ji}^{LC} + \rho\Delta\lambda_{uj}^{LC}}{E_j}, \frac{e_{i,w} + \rho\Delta\lambda_{ji}^{LC}}{E_i})$$

This formula is based on the path weight definition and the observation that extending a path by one more link only adds to the power consumption by the sender and the receiver of the link. The pseudo-code for the algorithm is given below.

Extended Bellman-Ford (EBF) Algorithm.

(1)   for each node $i \in N$
        $PATH(i) = \emptyset$
        for each input link $(j, i) \in L$
        $Weight(p_{si}(j)) = 0$
(2)   for $k = 1$ to $|N| - 1$
        for each link $(j, i) \in L$
        for each path $p_{sj}(u) \in PATH(j)$
        if $Weight(p_{sj}(u) + (j, i)) < Weight(p_{si}(j))$,
        then
        replace $p_{si}(j)$ with path $p_{si}(u) + (j, i)$.
(3)   return $p_{sd}(i)$ whose weight is the maximal among all paths in $PATH(d)$.

The original Bellman-Ford algorithm takes $O(n^3)$ time where $n = |N|$ is the number of nodes in the network. In the Extended Bellman-Ford algorithm, the maximum number of input links of each node is n. So, the time complexity of EBF is $O(n^4)$.

THEOREM 4.1. *EBF algorithm returns the weighted shortest path for w.*
Proof. Proof is presented in Appendix A. □

4.4. Solution for problem 3.3. The objective function in this problem is the rate of total energy consumption at all nodes in the network when a link cover mode is in place. As we know, in link cover mode, the end-to-end flow in each operation mode must be routed individually. So we need to take the two-level flow rerouting approach introduced in Section IV(C).

When an end-to-end flow w is selected for rerouting, we intend to route it in such a way that increases the aggregate energy consumption rate to the minimal. Assuming that we know all the routes between the source node and destination node of the flow, we may use Equation (4) to evaluate the would-be increase of traffic rate on each link if a particular route were to be assigned to the flow. Observe that an increase of traffic rate $\Delta\lambda_{ij}^{LC}$ on link (i, j) contributes $(\tau + \rho) * \Delta\lambda_{ij}^{LC}$ to the aggregate energy consumption rate. So, if we assign each link (i, j) with weight $\Delta\lambda_{ij}^{LC}$, the most energy conserving path for w will be the weighted shortest path.

5. Performance evaluation. In this section, we present the results of simulations we conducted for evaluating the performance of two traffic padding schemes.

For the simulation, we assumed a network with two operation modes and generated the end-to-end flow traffic pattern in each mode randomly. As we know, each end-to-end flow is specified by a (source, destination) tuple and an average flow traffic rate. We picked the endpoints of each flow randomly from the set of nodes and generated a random number within a given range as the flow rate. In all our experiments, the number of flows in each mode is 300.

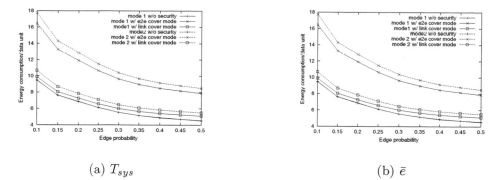

(a) T_{sys} (b) $\bar{e}$

FIG. 5.1. *Absolute values of performance metrics in 20-node random networks ($E_i = 10^7, \rho = 1, \tau = 2$)*

To generate different network topologies, we used the GT-ITM topology generator [26] software that generates connected random graphs. Given the number of nodes, a random graph was generated by adding a duplex link between any pair of nodes with a probability p. We varied the value of p from 0.1 to 0.5. Intuitively, $p = 0.1$ produces a sparse graph and $p = 0.5$ produces a dense graph.

At initial time, all nodes were assumed to have same energy conserve – thus E_i was independent of i. We assumed that $E_i = 10^7$ energy units, $\rho = 1$ energy unit/data unit and $\tau = 2$ energy units/data unit.

In the first experiment, we fixed the number of nodes to 20 and changed the network topology by changing the edge probability. The end-to-end flow traffic patterns in two operation modes are generated in such a way that all flow traffic rates fall into the range [1..100] data units/sec. In Fig. 5.1(a), we plot T_{sys} as a function of edge probability p. For the system lifetime in end-to-end cover mode, we used the algorithm in Section 4.2 to find a routing solution for all end-to-end flows. And we used the same algorithm when we derived the would-be system lifetimes if system were to stay in the first operation mode or the second operation mode respectively. For the system lifetime in link cover mode, we used the algorithm in Section 4.3. In our implementation of the FD-based algorithms, flows were selected in sequence. In Fig. 5.1(b), we plot $\bar{e}$ as a function of edge probability p. We plot both the values of $\bar{c}$ when network was in a cover mode and that when network was not in a cover mode. As we pointed out, $\bar{c}$ was related to the current operation mode. To obtain those values, we used the shortest path routing algorithm and the heuristic routing algorithm in Section 4.4. In the figure, the two lines representing $\bar{e}(1)$ and $\bar{e}(2)$, the minimal energy consumption per unit data delivered in each operation mode when no cover mode was in use, overlap. For each point in Fig. 5.1(a) and Fig. 5.1(b), we ran the simulation for 20 times and plot the averaged result.

From the figures, we observe that when edge probability increases, the system lifetime is extended and the average energy consumption/data unit decreases

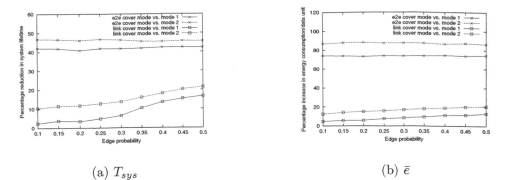

(a) T_{sys} (b) $\bar{e}$

FIG. 5.2. *Percentage of performance degradation in 20-node random networks($E_i =$* $10^7, \rho = 1, \tau = 2$)

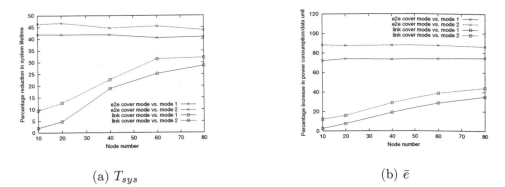

(a) T_{sys} (b) $\bar{e}$

FIG. 5.3. *Percentage of performance degradation in random networks with different number of nodes ($p = 0.25, E_i = 10^7, \rho = 1, \tau = 2$)*

in all cases. This is not surprising because in denser networks, more routes are available between each node pair for the system to choose from. So there is a better chance to get the initial routing solution improved.

Our major concern is the performance degradation in the system after cover mode was implemented. Fig. 5.2 illustrates the percentage reduction in T_{sys} and the percentage increase in $\bar{e}$ after using different cover modes. We can see that if end-to-end cover mode was used, there would be a 40% reduction in the system lifetime or a 70% increase in the average energy consumption/data unit. On the other hand, the system lifetime reduction in link cover mode is in the 2-20% range and the increase in the average energy consumption/data unit is less than 20%. So, link cover mode is much more power conserving than end-to-end cover mode.

In our second experiment, we fixed the edge probability p to 0.25 and changed the network size in terms of number of nodes. The percentage reduction in T_{sys} and the percentage increase in $\bar{e}$ are demonstrated in Fig. 5.3. It is interesting to observe that when the network becomes "larger", the per-

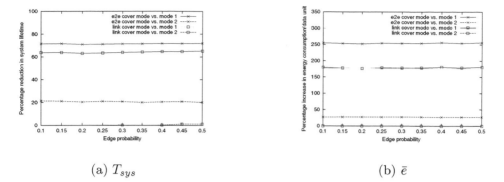

(a) T_{sys} (b) $\bar{e}$

FIG. 5.4. *Percentage of performance degradation in 20-node random networks with operation modes generated differently ($p = 0.25, E_i = 10^7, \rho = 1, \tau = 2$)*

formance of end-to-end cover mode and link cover mode approaches each other. In other words, the link cover mode performs worse in larger networks than in smaller networks. Remember that when system searches for the "best" routing solution that leads to the "optimal" link cover mode, it shifts some end-to-end flows away from their shortest hop paths to reduce the traffic rates on some congested links. In larger networks, the alternative paths found for these flows are usually longer than the paths found in smaller networks with same edge probability, i.e. containing more nodes and links, which increases the possibility of perturbing the optimality of other existing paths. So the correlation among the flows will have more impact on the flow path selection in larger networks than it does in smaller networks.

In our third experiment, we fixed the number of nodes to 20 and changed the edge probability as in the first experiment. But we generated two operation modes differently in that the average traffic rates of end-to-end flows in mode 1 were in range [1..50] data units/sec whereas the flow traffic rates in mode 2 were in range [1..150] data units/sec. So the network was more lightly loaded in mode 1 than in mode 2. Simulation results plotted in Fig. 5.4 show that the system lifetime achieved in link cover mode was even longer than that achieved in mode 2. Implementing link cover mode even produced a better performance than the original operation mode. This result was counter-intuitive. A likely reason is that our heuristic algorithm did not find the global optimal solution in some cases. A second observation we can make is that the relative performance degradation of cover mode against mode 1 was much higher than that against mode 2, which implies that if the network spents most of the time in mode 1, the cost of preventing traffic analysis will be extremely high. But, if the network usually stays in mode 2 and switches to mode 1 occasionally, implementing a cover mode will be cost effective.

6. Related work. Newman-Wolfe and Venkatraman proposed a security scheme for hiding end-to-end flow traffic pattern[19]. In the proposed scheme, both traffic padding and traffic rerouting techniques are utilized. The goal of the scheme is to present to the intruder a neutral traffic pattern which appears as equal traffic load on all end-to-end flows. The performance analysis of this scheme is given in [20, 24].

Radosavljevic and Hajek also investigated the problem of hiding end-to-end flow traffic patterns in packet radio networks [21]. The solution they proposed is to develop a fixed node transmission schedule which is independent of any end-to-end flow traffic demands. The reduction of throughput by using this scheme was analyzed.

We presented some preliminary results related to the problem addressed in this paper in [13] and [14]. In [13], the link traffic padding scheme was first proposed. This paper significantly extends on our preliminary work.

Optimal routing problem has attracted persistent interests of researchers in decades. The techniques proposed have a wide spectrum. In addition to the flow deviation method we used in this paper, Gavish and Hantler [8] and Lin and Yee [18] all applied dual methods based on Lagrangean relaxation to solve this programming problem. Simulated annealing was first used in [25] to cope with this problem.

7. Conclusions. This paper examines two types of traffic padding schemes, end-to-end traffic padding and link traffic padding, used to generate dummy traffic and prevent malicious traffic analysis. We provide theoretical analysis on the performance of the produced traffic cover modes with respect to energy consumption. Simulation results indicate that end-to-end cover mode generally performs worse than link cover mode, but in large networks, the two approaches yield similar energy overheads. It was also shown that when the traffic demands are skewed among the operation modes, implementing this security scheme may mean unacceptably high performance degradation.

For the future work, we plan to implement the two traffic padding schemes in a testbed wireless ad hoc network. An important characteristic of wireless ad hoc network is dynamical change of topology. From the security standpoint, end-to-end cover mode is independent of the actual network topology. But as we have shown in the paper, the feasibility of a cover mode depends on its performance on energy saving. Our FD-based routing algorithm requires global knowledge of topology which is costly to obtain in wireless ad hoc network. We will focus on developing distributed routing algorithm. It is still not clear how link cover mode should be defined when network topology might change, because operation mode change is not the only event that triggers the change of link flow traffic pattern.

REFERENCES

[1] O. BERG, T. BERG, S. HAAVIK, J. HJELMSTAD, AND R. SKAUG, *Spread Spectrum in Mobile Communication*, IEEE, 1998.
[2] D. BERTSEKAS AND R. GALLAGER, *Data Networks (Second edition)*, Prentice Hall, 1992.
[3] J.-H. CHANG AND L. TASSIULAS, *Energy conserving routing in wireless ad-hoc networks*, in INFOCOM 2000, Apr. 2000.

[4] C. CHIASSERINI AND R. RAO, *A traffic control scheme to optimize the battery pulsed discharge*, in MilCom'99, Nov. 1999.

[5] T. H. CORMEN, C. E. LEISERSON, AND R. L. RIVEST, *Introduction to Algorithms*, The MIT Press, 1990.

[6] DARPA, *Research challenges in high confidence networking*, http://www.darpa.mil/ito/research/hcn/problems.html, July 1998.

[7] M. R. GAREY AND D. S. JOHNSON, *Computers and Intractability*, W. H. Freeman and Company, New York, 1979.

[8] B. GAVISH AND S. L. HANTLER, *An algorithm for optimal route selection in sna networks*, IEEE Trans. Commun., COM-31, (1983), pp. 1154–1161.

[9] Y. GUAN, X. FU, R. BETTATI, AND W. ZHAO, *Efficient traffic camouflaging in mission-critical qos-guaranteed networks*, in IEEE Information Assurance and Security Workshop, June 2000.

[10] Y. GUAN, X. FU, D. XUAN, P. SHENOY, R. BETTATI, AND W. ZHAO, *Netcamo: Camouflaging network traffic for qos-guaranteed mission critical applications*, IEEE/ACM Transactions on System, Man, and Cybernetics, (to appear).

[11] Y. GUAN, C. LI, D. XUAN, R. BETTATI, AND W. ZHAO, *Preventing traffic analysis for real-time communication networks*, in MilCom'99, Nov. 1999, pp. 744–750.

[12] IETF MANET WORKING GROUP, *Mobile ad-hoc networks*. http://www.ietf.org/html.charters/manet-charter.html.

[13] S. JIANG, N. H. VAIDYA, AND W. ZHAO, *Routing in packet radio networks to prevent traffic analysis*, in IEEE Information Assurance and Security Workshop, June 2000.

[14] ———, *Preventing traffic analysis in packet radio networks*, in DARPA Information Survivability Conference and Exposition (DISCEX), May 2001.

[15] D. JOHNSON AND D. A. MALTZ, *Dynamic source routing in ad hoc wireless networks*, in Mobile Computing, T. Imielinski and H. Korth, eds., Kluwere Academic Publishers, 1994.

[16] R. KRAVETS, K. SCHWAN, AND K. CALVERT, *Power-aware communication for mobile computers*, in International Workshop on Mobile Multimedia Communications(MoMuc'99), 1999.

[17] M. G. L. FRATTA AND L. KLEINROCK, *The flow deviation method: an approach to store and-forward communication network design*, Networks, 3 (1973), pp. 97–133.

[18] F. LIN AND J. WANG, *Minimax open shortest path first routing algorithms in networks supporting the smds service*, in International Conference on Communications(ICC'93), May 1993.

[19] R. E. NEWMAN-WOLFE AND B. R. VENKATRAMAN, *High level prevention of traffic analysis*, in Seventh Annual Computer Security and Applications Conference, Dec. 1991.

[20] ———, *Performance analysis of a method for high level prevention of traffic analysis*, in Eighth Annual Computer Security and Applications Conference, Nov. 1992.

[21] B. RADOSAVLJEVIC AND B. HAJEK, *Hiding traffic flow in communication networks*, in MilCom'92, Oct. 1992.

[22] S. SINGH, M. WOO, AND C. S. RAGHAVENDRA, *Power-aware routing in mobile ad hoc networks*, in ACM/IEEE International Conference on Mobile Computing and Networking(MobiCom'98), 1998.

[23] W. STALLINGS, *Local & Metropolitan Area Networks (Fifth edition)*, Prentice Hall, 1996.

[24] B. R. VENKATRAMAN AND R. E. NEWMAN-WOLFE, *Performance analysis of a method for high level prevention of traffic analysis using measurements from a campus network*, in Tenth Annual Computer Security and Applications Conference, Dec. 1994.

[25] J.-L. W. Y.-J. CHANG AND H.-J. HU, *Optimal virtual circuit routing in computer networks*, IEE Proceedings I: Communications, Speech and Vision, 139 (1992).

[26] E. ZEGURA, *Modeling topology of large internetworks*. http://www.cc.gatech.edu/fac/Ellen.Zegura/graphs.html.

Appendix A. Proof of Theorem 4.1.

We prove by induction. Assuming that before k−th iteration, $PATH(i)$ contains the optimal paths from node s to node i (through different input links

Shu Jiang and Nitin H. Vaidya and Wei Zhao

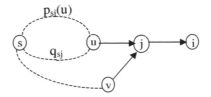

FIG. A.1. *Proof of Theorem 4.1*

at node i) with no more than $k - 1$ hops, we prove that after k–th iteration, $PATH(i)$ contains the optimal paths with no more than k hops. From the algorithm, the path $p_{si}(j)$ in $PATH(i)$ is found by calculating the weights of all paths $p_{sj}(u) + (j, i)$ where $p_{sj}(u)$ is a path in $PATH(j)$ and choosing the one with minimal weight. We now prove two facts.

Fact 1: $p_{si}(j)$ is optimal. Let q_{sj} be any a path from s to j. Assume that u is the last node before j on path q_{sj}(See Fig. A.1). Then the weight of path $q_{sj} + (j, i)$ can be computed by using the formula (6). If we denote c_1 as $\frac{e_{j,w} + \tau \Delta \lambda_{ji}^{LC}, + \rho \Delta \lambda_{uj}^{LC}}{E_j}$ and c_2 as $\frac{e_{i,w} + \rho \Delta \lambda_{ji}^{LC}}{E_i}$ for clarity, then we have

(1) $$Weight(q_{sj} + (j, i)) = \max(Weight(q_{sj}), c_1, c_2).$$

As we know, the weight of path $p_{sj}(u) + (u, v)$ has similar form:

(2) $$Weight(p_{sj}(u) + (u, v)) = \max(Weight(p_{sj}(u)), c_1, c_2)$$

Since $Weight(q_{sj}) \geq Weight(p_{sj}(u))$, then the following inequalities must be true.

(3) $$Weight(q_{sj} + (j, i)) \geq Weight(p_{sj}(u) + (u, v))$$
(4) $$\geq Weight(p_{si}(j)).$$

Fact 2: $p_{si}(j)$ contains no more than k hops. The portion of the path from s to j contains no more than $k - 1$ hops. The last link (j, i) contributes one hop. So the number of hops in $p_{si}(j)$ cannot be more than k.

After $|N| - 1$ iterations, $PATH(d)$ contains the optimal paths from s to d through different input links and each contains no more than $|N| - 1$ hops. Since there are no negative links, the optimal path cannot have more than $|N| - 1$ hops. In other words, the path in $PATH(d)$ with minimal weight is just the optimal path from s to d. This concludes the proof of the theorem.   □

INTRUSION DETECTION AND RESPONSE FOR REAL-TIME DISTRIBUTED NAVAL SYSTEMS

B. L. CHAPPELL, G. A. FINK, D. T. MARLOW, AND K. F. O'DONOGHUE*

Abstract. Information security in naval environments is becoming increasingly important with the move towards distributed engineering and computing, increased automation, and systems based upon non-developmental items (NDI). Naval applications have a broad range of communication timing requirements, from tens of seconds to sub-seconds. For example, the communication between geographically dispersed operational sites may require responses in the seconds or tens of seconds range, while the communication between applications in a shipboard combat system that are responsible for targeting weapons have much more constrained timing requirements. Additionally, there are mission critical applications that have hard real-time requirements in which the reception of data outside of specific timing limits results in system failure, as well as mission critical applications with near real-time requirements that can tolerate a wider boundary of communication response times. The integration of information security services in such an environment invariably conflicts with the timing requirements of these applications. However, security services are arguably needed most in environments with the tightest communication requirements (e.g., while engaging hostile targets). NSWC-DD has begun evaluating the applicability of Intrusion Detection Systems (IDS) in naval environments. This paper describes current security architectures of naval platforms, potential future architectures, and desirable features of an IDS that may be integrated into these architectures.

Key words. Intrusion Detection, Intrusion Tolerance, Intrusion Response Planning and Execution, Attach Strategy Analysis, Navy Shipboard Architecture

1. Introduction. Future shipboard naval platforms will consist of distributed computing systems composed of hundreds of processors connected by a network infrastructure. Applications with a wide range of performance requirements will execute on these platforms. There will be a mix of mission critical applications (e.g., navigation, sonar and radar processing, and weapons control) and non-mission critical, quality-of-life applications (e.g., email, web, and distributed entertainment video). The shipboard applications will have a combination of hard real-time requirements, soft real-time requirements, and non real-time requirements. For the purposes of this paper, an application with a hard real-time requirement cannot tolerate delays beyond a certain bound in receiving data. Receiving data outside this range results in application failure. An application with soft real-time requirements has a set of bounds in which the data is needed but which can still be used if delivered late. [1]

The design of future naval computing architectures is based upon non-developmental items, such as commercial-off-the-shelf products, in order to reduce cost. The move away from specialized components has resulted in many new challenges in the design and implementation process. Information security is an increasingly difficult challenge given the commercial-based components and

---

*System Research and Technology Department, Combat Systems Branch, Naval Surface Warfare Center, Dahlgren Division, Dahlgren, VA 22448-5100, U.S.A. (chappellbl, finkga, dmarlow, kodonog@nswc.navy.mil).

distributed nature of future systems. Information security requirements inherently conflict with the performance requirements of applications executing in a naval shipboard platform. This paper gives an overview of current and future computing and security architectures in naval shipboard platforms, and it describes the features of an intrusion detection and response system that are desirable with respect to this platform.

2. Naval Shipboard Computing Architectures. The performance requirements of a naval shipboard computing architectures differ from typical industry computing requirements. As mentioned previously, communication requirements between certain distributed applications are much more stringent than those of typical commercial applications. For example, for ship self-defense systems, the timeline required to process and correlate radar information and provide it to a weapons control subsystem is quite small and fixed. If the information is not provided to the weapons control subsystem within the timeline, then the system fails. For example, if an incoming air threat is not intercepted and destroyed, then the ship will likely sustain damage. Additionally, a naval shipboard computing architecture operates in a demanding and sometimes hostile environment. The computing and communication systems must be able to withstand extreme environmental conditions as well as gracefully degrade in the event of damage. Fault detection and recovery mechanisms must be present within the system. For example, if an information warfare attack disables a mission critical database server, there should be mechanisms available for the restoration of the mission critical services provided by the database server.

In addition to stringent performance requirements, shipboard systems operate in an environment with specific off-board communication requirements. A naval vessel is often deployed as a member of a group of ships. Communications with other members of the group of ships (battle group) are required. In order for the commander of the battle group to maintain a cohesive view of the operational environment, sensor data information must be exchanged and correlated between different ships of the battle group, as well as with land-based sites. Off-board communications of a ship are sent and received across low bandwidth links. The information exchanged across these links is often mission critical, and it is important to ensure that data has not been tampered with or modified during transit.

2.1. Legacy Shipboard Computing Architectures. The previous shipboard computing platforms were composed of highly specialized systems interconnected via point-to-point interconnections. The processing occurred in centralized locations, and there was limited communication between applications. Although there were off-board communications to systems aboard other ships, there was very little, if any, data exchanged with public networks, such as the Internet. The resulting architecture did not have many of the inherent information security vulnerabilities present in current ship designs.

Both the operating system and the user interface used were unique to the shipboard computers that required special training to operate. As a result, it was much more difficult for potential adversaries to exploit vulnerabilities even if they were to manage to gain external access to a shipboard system.

2.2. Requirements of Future Shipboard Computing Architectures.
Numerous requirements for future naval shipboard platforms have necessitated a change from a centralized, point-to-point architecture to a distributed, LAN-based architecture. The primary goals of this change are: reduced lifecycle cost, reduced manning, meeting new threats, improved quality of life for the sailor, and ability to participate in multinational coalitions.

Reduced lifecycle cost is the overarching goal that drives shipboard architecture toward the future. With the shrinking DoD budgets of the past several years, the Navy cannot afford to design, deploy, and maintain architectures based on highly specialized, non-commercial equipment. The use of NDI products is encouraged, and in general, only applications with unique requirements will justify the use of a non-commercial system.

Previous naval shipboard architectures used a stove-piped design, as shown in Figure 2.1. Shipboard systems were developed to meet specific operational requirements. As a result, system engineers independently selected or, in some cases, built their own Engineering Base, that is, their own system and software architectures, including networks, computers, operating systems, interface standards, middleware, consoles, etc. These "stove-piped" systems were then integrated aboard a ship. This was typically performed through a costly process of producing an Interface Design Specification among the various systems. In many cases, the cost and effort associated with integrating these systems was not affordable, resulting in entirely stand-alone systems that required human intervention to transfer information or data between the systems. This resulted in an inconsistent architecture that was difficult to scale and maintain. Also, computing and communication resources could not be easily shared between subsystems. Total ship computing is an attempt to reduce the number of stove-piped systems and allow more efficient use of all the ship's computing resources. But, it challenges traditional security methods that relied upon a physical air-gap between systems of differing classification level.

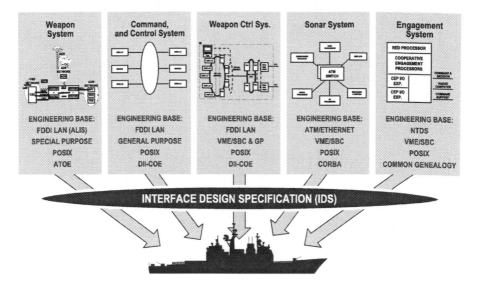

FIG. 2.1. *A stove-piped computing architecture.*

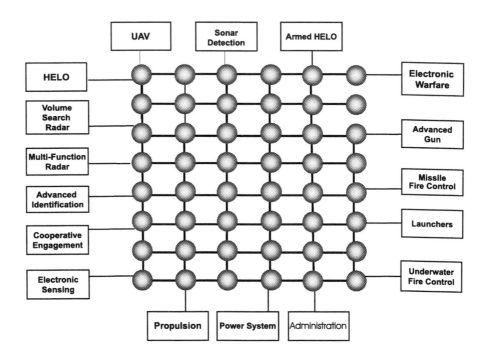

FIG. 2.2. *A total ship computing architecture.*

Total ship computing is a methodology currently being investigated to reduce life cycle costs while maintaining the needed performance. Total ship computing provides a means pooling all the ship's distributed computing resources into a virtual computing cluster that can be called upon to process all applications, as shown in Figure 2.2. When an application needs computing resources, it simply accesses a portion of the distributed resources by making a request to a resource manager. The resource manager is responsible for determining the appropriate amount of computing resources based upon the application's requirements, the priority of the application, and the available pool of resources. [2]

Reduced manning, another cost saving objective, will increase the amount of automation of tasks that previously required a man-in-the-loop. The goal is to drastically reduce the number of sailors required to successfully carry out the ship's mission. The resource manager will play a key role in reducing manning. The ship's resource manager will be responsible for allocating and reconfiguration of computing resources as resource availability changes. Modifications in resource allocations will occur based on changing mission requirements, system status (e.g. potential battle damage), maintenance schedules, and user requirements. The security architecture of the ship and the resource management architecture need to co-exist and supplement one another.

The environment in which U.S. Navy ships must conduct operations is continually changing. New threats must be dealt with, specifically when more sophisticated weapons are deployed by adversaries. As the environment changes and new threats appear, the computing and communications requirements become stricter.

Another objective of future naval platforms is improved the quality of life for the sailor. This goal drives the architecture because of the high cost of personnel turnover and training. An improved quality of life for the sailor is anticipated as being key to personnel retention. One aspect of this is to expand the sailor's ability to keep in touch with the civilian world with access to email, video entertainment, and web based content. While there will not likely be a direct connection between the ship and the Internet, information that originates from the Internet will likely be brought onboard the ship's computer systems. For example, a land-based Network Operations Center (NOC) may serve as an intermediate link for the ship's systems to reach the Internet. This land-based NOC may provide email and web based services to applications aboard the ship. This, in combination with the fact that future naval computing platforms will likely be based upon commercial equipment, raises many of the same information security concerns that the corporate world must deal with, including intrusion detection and response.

Finally, in today's political reality US ships must participate in Allied and coalition operations with diverse partners. Existing naval systems were not designed with information sharing in mind, especially in situations where the whole spectrum of trust is exercised. Some coalition partners will be highly trusted while others may not be allies at all. Information sharing is required in these environments, but this capability opens up possibilities for hostile access.

3. Security Architectures. Naval shipboard computing architecture presents a number of security challenges that need to be addressed. One is the migration from stove-piped security architecture based upon physical separation of systems according to classification level to a security architecture that can be integrated into a total ship computing architecture, perhaps based on multi-level security (MLS) or multi-security level (MSL) initiatives.

Another security challenge is the issue of the availability of mission critical computing resources. Adversaries could hijack mission critical systems denying service and jeopardizing the mission. The adversary may also obtain sensitive or classified data. These threats should be considered during the design of the architecture. It is very difficult to keep secrets in a distributed computing architecture that is based upon the premise of applications sharing data with one another.

3.1. Goals of Security Architecture. The security architecture of a shipboard platform must support the multiple missions of the ship and not inhibit the successful completion of any mission. A primary goal of any shipboard security architecture is to ensure that only properly authenticated personnel and applications have access to computing resources and data they need, when they need it. It is difficult to achieve a proper balance of security and performance. For example, strong security measures may be taken to ensure that confidential data remains hidden from unauthorized personnel or applications. However, if these same security measures prevent the properly cleared personnel or applications from obtaining this data or needed resources, then the security architecture is worthless.

Likewise, the performance of an intrusion detection system must be balanced in that both "false positives" and "false negatives" are minimized. A system that reports an intrusion when none exists, a false positive will likely eventually be turned off or ignored. And, a system that does not detect an actual intrusion can be just as ineffective. In addition, it is desirable that an intrusion be detected in time for a response to be formulated that will prevent mission critical resources or data from being neutralized. Also, to support the graceful degradation of performance in the event of an information warfare attack, a security architecture should allow continued operation during and after the attack. Often, a response to an intrusion is to block communications from the source computer or network. If access to networks is shutoff during an attack, the platform may not be able to carry out its mission. Thus, a more sophisticated response will often be required. The remainder of this section discusses how an intrusion detection and response system may be used in currently deployed shipboard computing architectures as well as potential future architectures.

3.2. Physically Separated Enclaves. Security architectures of previously deployed ship classes are based on protection through physical separation, as shown in Figure 3.1. For each security level present in the architecture, a physically distinct set of computing and communication resources is implemented.

Each system attached to a particular enclave executes in a "system-high" mode of operation. In other words, each system, and all applications present on each system, must be accredited to operate in the highest security classification supported by that enclave. There is no automated method of sharing data between the applications with different classification levels. In order to transfer data from the level one enclave to the level two enclave, a deliberate decision must be made to upgrade or downgrade the data, and the data must be physically carried by some media to the other enclave (e.g., on a floppy diskette). The computing resources of each enclave reside on a shared media. This security architecture can easily be implemented in a stove-piped system, but since it partitions resources based upon classification level, it conflicts with the goal of a total ship computing architecture.

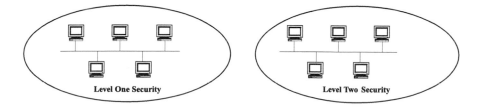

FIG. 3.1. *Physically Separated Enclaves*

In this type of architecture, an IDS could be deployed in any enclave where the threat of malicious activity warrants it. For example, an IDS may be needed in an enclave that has an external data link. Likewise, an IDS may be used on an enclave that contains highly sensitive data, and the threat of a malicious insider accessing data or resources without authorization is present.

3.3. Separate Enclaves with Secure Gateway Connections. In an effort to automate the sharing of data between computing enclaves based on classification levels, secure communication devices may be added in the design of the security architecture, as shown in Figure 3.2. These devices allow for regulated communication between separate enclaves. For example, some classes of data may be allowed to flow from a higher security level to a lower security level as illustrated in the figure, and vice-versa. Essentially, this architecture provides a limited form of automated data transfer between enclaves at different classification levels. Although an improvement over physical separation, computing resources are still partitioned which results in limitations in achieving a total ship computing architecture. In this type of architecture, it may be sensible to deploy an IDS on the unclassified backbone, in each enclave, or perhaps in both places.

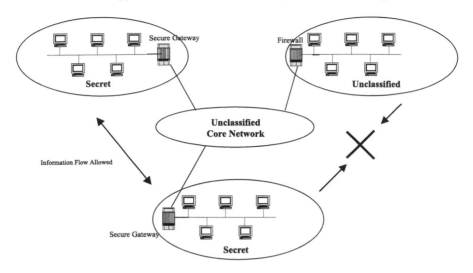

FIG. 3.2. *Separated Enclaves connected via Security Gateways*

3.4. Integrated Security Architecture. In order to fully support the distributed architecture described in section 2.3, the method of providing security functionality through the physical isolation of computing and communication resources must end. Instead of separating resources based upon classification levels, it is the information that should be separated. In Figure 3.3, a notional architecture is shown based on this assertion.

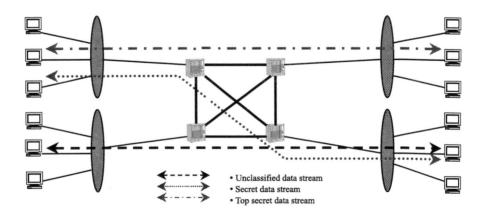

FIG. 3.3. *Integrated Security Architecture*

This type of security architecture may provide the most challenges of deploying a successful IDS system. The security architectures described in the previous two sections are either in use today or are based upon accreditable technology. The architecture described in this section is notional. In addition to the technical challenges involved, current DoD security policies will not allow this type of system to be accredited.

4. Challenges to an Intrusion Detection and Response System.
There are several challenges when attempting to implement an effective intrusion detection system. Both the frequency and sophistication of attacks upon the Internet infrastructure have increased in the last few years. [3] This section describes some of the challenges of deploying an intrusion detection system (IDS) or an intrusion detection and response system (IDRS) successfully in a naval shipboard environment. These challenges may also apply to a broader environment, but the focus is upon the naval environment.

4.1. Sophistication of Potential Adversaries.
The goals of adversaries of the U.S. Navy are quite similar to those of attacks carried out on the general Internet. One goal may be to disrupt mission critical resources aboard a ship in order to deny their use in the successful completion of the ship's mission. Another goal may be to steal information contained aboard the ship's systems in order to plan and execute a successful denial of service attack or obtain nation-security level secrets.

The skill of hostile or malicious adversaries attempting to intrude upon naval systems varies over a wide range. Since commercial equipment will become more prevalent in future designs, the same vulnerabilities and weaknesses present in the commercial marketplace will be present aboard a ship. Also, the quality of life services require that some type of connection to the Internet be present. As a result, an IDRS must be capable of detecting and responding to the type of attacks common in today's Internet. Often, relatively unskilled adversaries gain access to tools used to automate attacks against known vulnerabilities that are shared in the hacker community.

On the other end of the spectrum are highly skilled, perhaps professional, adversaries that may be sponsored by nation-states to carry out attacks against the U.S. Government or Department of Defense. Detecting and responding to this activity generally is much more difficult because previously unknown attacks may be used. Commercial intrusion detection systems perform well in the detection of known attacks, but most do not detect previously unknown attacks or derive the intentions of an adversary.

4.2. Detection Mechanism.
IDS technology differentiates between legitimate traffic and attacks using knowledge of either the normal operation of the system being protected (anomaly-based ID) or with a database of known attack profiles (signature-based ID). Some IDSs may use both. The problem is that normal behavior is hard to characterize because it is dynamic in most environments. The behavior of systems in a shipboard environment is somewhat static, but depending upon the environment and current mission, the behavior can change. Signature-based IDSs also have disadvantages. For example, attack signatures only cover known attacks; they can do nothing about new attacks or attacks handcrafted to look normal. Anomaly-based systems typically have

a higher false-positive detection rate (meaning they classify legitimate behavior as an attack) while signature-based IDSs generally have higher false-negative rates (meaning that some unknown attacks were missed). While the actual false-positive rate of an IDS can be measured by the number of times legitimate behavior is classified as an intrusion, the true false-negative rate in a deployed system can never be known because those attacks are undetected.

Signature-based IDSs are by far more widely deployed and marketed. These systems are essentially packet analyzers that look for strings of data within packets that match known attack strings. The problem is that the same attack can be encoded in so many ways that detecting all of them is virtually impossible. For instance, web servers can understand data sent as normal text or encoded in hexadecimal, and terminals can be set to expect EBCIDIC encoded strings instead of standard ASCII. Even simple things like inserting backspaces or extra spaces in command lines can confuse an IDS. So, an adversary who is a bad typist may actually have more success subverting an IDS by virtue of his many mistakes. Modern IDSs have overcome some of these simpler camouflage methods, but they incur a certain performance penalty to do so.

4.3. Capability to Respond to Intrusions. Most commercial IDSs have limited, if any, capabilities to respond to an intrusion within a hard real-time deadline of a navy shipboard system. [4,5,6] In a shipboard environment, it is necessary to quickly respond to an attack in order to ensure that the mission critical resources and data are protected. A response may be as simple as modifying an access list on a firewall to block the attack, as in most commercial IDSs. Or, the response may be more sophisticated in which the mission critical applications executing on a compromised system are moved to other resources. [7] If the response does not occur in time to ensure that the mission critical applications obtain the resources required to successfully execute, then the IDRS has failed.

4.4. Real-time Performance. Today's networks operate at gigabit speeds, 100 to 1000 times faster than when intrusion detection technology was first conceived. The time required to analyze and correlate the network and host data, determine an attack has occurred, formulate a response, and execute the response is limited. As mentioned earlier, in a shipboard computing environment, mission critical, hard and soft real-time timelines exist. If the time from detecting an attack to responding to an attack violates these timelines, a mission critical application may fail. The performance of any IDS deployed aboard a ship is vital.

Also, It is difficult to collect and store the amount of data that typically traverses today's networks without running out of storage. Supposing an IDS was deployed on a network with an average traffic load of 100 Mbit/sec. That means the system could fill a megabyte of disk space every eight seconds. This system would fill a standard 36 gigabyte drive every three days of continuous operation. An IDS must distinguish among dead-normal traffic, suspicious traffic, and attack traffic. Only the latter two types should be stored. Suspicious traffic must be continually mined for correlation to any type of attack and can be discarded if it is determined to be normal. Attacks may take place over a long period of time specifically to defeat an IDS, so data must be retained until the entire attack can be seen. The problem is establishing rules about what makes a packet suspicious. Rules that are too stringent will discard too much and make analysis difficult or impossible. Rules that are too lax will store too much data and make analysis slow. Finding the right rule set is a matter of tuning that takes a certain amount of expertise and knowledge about the network where an IDS is operating.

A competent adversary can use this dilemma against an IDS. If they suspect an IDS is guarding the system, they can flood the system with suspicious data until the IDS either depletes storage space or processing power. The ship's personnel may be aware that an attack is underway, but the IDS could not formulate a response. Also, it is likely that if an information warfare attack such as this is carried out, it will occur when mission critical resources are needed the most. For example, a hostile force may preface an air or undersea attack against a battle force with an information warfare attack in order to increase the chance of a successful attack. The IDS will consume valuable computing and communication resources aboard the ship in response to the attack that could otherwise be dedicated other mission critical ship defense applications.

4.5. Switched Networks. Future shipboard networks will not be flat, hub-based networks where all systems are on the same "wire." Switched networks now separate data into routing enclaves where the only data on the wire is what concerns the group of machines within an enclave. There are limited central locations where a single IDS appliance could be placed to observe all network traffic. Instead, individual IDSs may need to be placed within individual routing enclaves to watch only the packets visible within. While it is possible to use port mirroring to reflect all traffic into a single enclave where an IDS resides, this is an inefficient use of bandwidth, requires administrative maintenance, complicates the analysis of the data received by the IDS, and may overload the switch resources during high loads. Instead, it may be necessary to have a hierarchy of IDSs that all communicate to form a global view of the network, but even this has its complications. First, communication between IDSs requires them to break the silence that hides their presence. Second, the data exchanged would be candidate attack signatures or the like, very valuable to any adversary in the system. A secure communications channel between the IDSs may be required to avoid these problems, but this will add to the complexity of the security architecture.

4.6. Encryption. Encryption technology will most likely be used in future security architectures of shipboard environments. It may be prevalent throughout the platform, such as in the integrated architecture described in section 3.4, or it may only be used on the edges of an enclave architecture. In order to detect most intrusions, the IDS needs to have access to data contained in higher layer protocols. Encrypting this data limits the amount of intrusions an IDS can detect. Additionally, anomaly based IDSs must have access to the data at higher layers in order to compare it to the "known behavior" of the system.

The use of encryption is a major obstacle of deploying an intrusion detection and response system. Either the IDS must gain access to the encrypted data, or the security architecture must be designed in such a way that the use of encryption is limited. Neither solution may be practical.

4.7. Difficulty of Tracing Attacks. In addition to the purely technical, tactical-level problems listed above there are strategic and forensic issues with intrusions. Intrusions represent an excellent source of intelligence on enemy operations if they can be recorded with sufficient accuracy. Although this is not an immediate concern for the warfighter, intelligence analysts and higher echelons will have great interest in this dimension of intrusion detection. The primary challenge to this use of an IDS is that any adversary capable of being a serious threat is easily able to hide his real identity by using incorrect return addresses within his data packets. IP routing does not have any standard way of tracing data back to its actual source. Adversaries can use special programs, proxy servers, and long trails of telnet sessions to increase the difficulty of tracing the attack. Typically, it takes quite a bit of forensic data over numerous episodes to track an adversary down to his actual local network. While this data is being gathered, correlated, and analyzed, the adversary may gain access to a system, deny service to legitimate users, or steal important data. The best defense against spoofing is rapid correlation of potential attack sessions. Sharing forensic data among separate sites can help reduce correlation times but nothing can yet be done to address the root of the problem. Authenticated routing protocols could reduce this problem, but the amount of time before these protocols are deployed (if ever) is unknown.

5. Conclusions. This paper has discussed notional security architectures that may be appropriate for use in a shipboard environment. Additionally, the integration of an intrusion detection and response system into the potential architectures was discussed, along with the desired features of such a system.

The current state of commercial intrusion detection systems may not be suitable for use in a naval shipboard computing environment. The majority of commercial products do not support more than simplistic response mechanisms. Most commercial systems are signature-based which do not detect previously unknown attacks. Also, it is questionable whether or not the performance of current systems will satisfy the performance requirements of naval shipboard architectures that must support both hard and soft real-time applications.

REFERENCES

[1] R. HARRISON, *Hard, Soft, Hybrid real-time systems and their uses*, Panel Discussion at NATO Advanced Study Institute on Real-time Computing, October 8th, 1992.
[2] L. R. WELCH, M. W. MASTERS, L. A. MADDEN, D. T. MARLOW, P. M. IREY IV, P. V. WERME, B. A. SHIRAZI, *A Distributed System Reference Architecture for Adaptive QoS and Resource Management*, Lecture Notes in Computer Science 1586

- IPPS/SDPD '99 Workshops - Parallel and Distributed Processing, 1316-1325, Springer-Verlag, 1999.

[3] R. PETHIA, *Internet Security Trends*, Software Engineering Institute Report, Carnegie-Mellon University, February, 2001.

[4] *NFR IDA Users Guide 5.0*, Network Flight Recorder, 2000.

[5] *Cisco Secure Intrusion Detection System Version 2.2.1 User Guide*, Cisco Systems, 2001.

[6] B. YOCOM, K. BROWN, AND D. VAN DERVEER, *Cisco offers wire-speed intrusion detection*, Network World, December 18th, 2000.

[7] B. TJADEN, L. WELCH, S. OSTERMANN, D. CHELBERG, R. BALUPARI, M. BYKOVA, A. MITCHELL, AND L. TONG, *SECURE-RM: Security and Resource Management for Dynamic Real-Time Systems*, Real-time System Security Minisymposium, Southern Conference on Computing (SCC 2000), The University of Southern Mississippi, October 26-28, 2000.

ENSURING INTEGRITY AND SERVICE AVAILABILITY IN A WEB-BASED CONTROL LABORATORY

SUNG-SOO LIM*, KIHWAL LEE†, AND LUI SHA‡

Abstract. The new millennium heralds the convergence of communication, computing and the intelligent control of the physical environment. However, as embedded devices being networked and becoming more accessible, the threat of security breaches also becomes increasingly serious. This paper focuses on how to ensure the integrity of the system, when mobile codes could contain not only bugs but also viruses.

Key words. security, real-time systems, static program analysis

1. Introduction. The rapid advancement of the Internet not only connects traditional servers and desktop computing systems, but also embedded devices. The vision of smart devices, cars, roads, houses and buildings working together intelligently prompted CACM to devote a special issue on "Embedding the Web" and predictions like: "the synergy fostered by interconnected embedded processors will make the much-touted digital convergence in desktop publishing and entertainment look like a blip in the history of computing technology." [4]. While it is difficult to know if such prediction will materialize as predicted, there is indeed an emerging trend towards connecting distributed embedded devices. The notion of smart home has been embraced by computing industry and smart house prototypes have become a major event in COMDEX. DARPA [23] has sponsored a series of programs on networked and embedded systems and EPRI has sponsored a five year, $30 million program to invest how better control the power generation and transmission in a deregulated environment [1]. On the educational front, the Internet enables not only distance learning but also web based engineering laboratory [25, 24].

Ensuring security in embedded systems is becoming increasingly important as they get connected to the Internet. Compared with traditional desktop systems, embedded devices have certain advantages as long as security is concerned. Embedded devices generally do not allow users to remotely login, nor do they support emails with attachments. Many of them will have a simple web interface but that is also more tightly controlled. However, they have to accept new codes across the web to support upgrades and evolutions. Such mobile code is a potential entry point for attacks. This situation is particularly acute in web based open engineering laboratory such as our Telelab [24], which allows users anywhere in the world to send in their software to control devices such as an inverted pendulum. Such experimental code could contain not only innocent

---
*School of Computer Science and Engineering, Seoul National University, Seoul 151-742, Korea (sslim@archi.snu.ac.kr).

†Department of Computer Science, University of Illinois, Urbana, IL 61801 (klee7@cs.uiuc.edu).

‡Department of Computer Science, University of Illinois, Urbana, IL 61801 (lrs@cs.uiuc.edu).

bugs but also malicious viruses. If left unchecked, they could not only interrupt the operations but also damage the physical devices.

Security problems in networked computer systems mainly consist of three areas: *confidentiality, integrity,* and *service availability.* The confidentiality is to protect data from unauthorized access using any authentication and digital signature method. The integrity is to prevent improper modification of any system component. The service availability (also referred to as assured service) is to prevent denial of service (DOS) attacks. The confidentiality has been extensively studied and the results of the studies can be applied to networked mission critical real-time system platforms without significant change of core concepts. Similarly, network level denial of service attacks can be handled by existing methods. On the other hand, the device level integrity and service availability problem in embedded real-time systems cannot be solved in the same way as those in general purpose systems for two reasons. First, security literature does not deal with malicious control codes, which was designed to interrupt the operation or to damage the devices within the given address space and execution privileges. Second, the capability management and resource isolation techniques for general purpose computing are often too resource consuming for embedded device applications.

In this paper, we focus on the integrity aspect of the security problems associated with accepting questionable control source codes in the context of our Telelab environment. The remainder of this paper is organized as follows: Section 2 introduces the Telelab, which is the base platform for our work. Section 3 describes the run-time checking of the Telelab. The static security check method, the main part of this paper, is described in Section 4. Section 5 shows the implementation details and some of the experimental results. Conclusions and future work are given in Section 6.

2. Telelab. As shown in Figure 2.1, Telelab allows users to access our control equipment, currently an inverted pendulum controlled by a computer, over the Internet without having to travel to a physically remote location in order to carry out experiments. Users can modify a given sample controller or write their own control software, upload it to the Telelab server, run it, and watch how well their software control the equipment via streaming video and the measurements sent back to them. A user is given feedback as to the state of their controller (running, failed), as well as the system states that led to the termination of their controller in the case of failure, in addition to visual feedback using streaming video.

In spite of innocent bugs, malicious control codes and viruses, Telelab must ensure integrity of the experimental environment and the availability of service at the device level. By "integrity" we mean that Telelab will not permit user's codes to modify any of its software components except the experimental control software component itself. In addition, Telelab protects the physical systems from potential user's abuse that could damage the motor or gears. By device level "service availability", we mean that the inverted pendulum (IP) must not

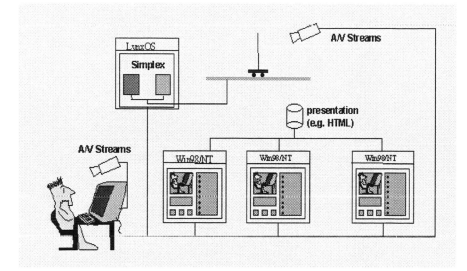

FIG. 2.1. *Telelab*

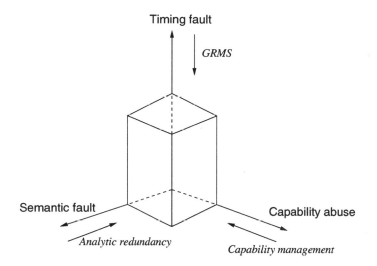

FIG. 2.2. *Vulnerability Model.*

fall down. Should this happen, a person must manually put the IP in an upright position at the middle of the track and then restart the Telelab. This interrupts the availability of the educational service. We do not want to put a person to watch and restart the Telelab all the time.

2.1. The Vulnerability Model. Since users can write any code as they wish and send it in and run it, our system can be attacked from three different angles. First, user code may contain an infinite busy loop that could potentially

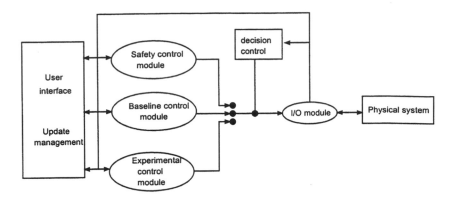

FIG. 2.3. *Simplex Architecture*

create a denial of service attack at the processor level. Second, user code may stay within its allocated capability but nevertheless contain innocent bugs or intentionally designed malicious controller that will ramp the IP down, inducing large oscillation, simply stop the control all together and let the IP to fall down naturally. Third, user code may abuse the allocated capability such as corrupting other modules' code or data or execute machine instructions disguised as data that will gain system management capabilities and then use such capability to destroy or alter Telelab structure.

In the early implementations of Telelab, resource sharing faults were protected by address space protection using UNIX processes. This works but is too expensive for embedded applications. Timing faults can be easily addressed by real time scheduling methods such as generalized rate monotonic scheduling (GRMS) [16]. There was no protection against user code's attempt to gain unauthorized capabilities in the early Telelab implementation.

Since the use of real-time scheduling technique to prevent timing faults is an established technology, we will not discuss this further in this paper. Because only source code is allowed and we control the compilation environment, it is not difficult to disallow users from making unauthorized system calls related to resource management and capability management. As a result, we will focus on the protection against the semantic faults and the use of static programming analysis techniques to achieve low cost resource sharing fault protection and to prevent users from gaining unauthorized capability by executing hidden or online generated machine instructions. Before we embark on detailed discussion, we will first provide an overview of the Telelab architecture. This will provide a useful context for discussion on the protection techniques.

2.2. The Telelab Architecture. When users submit their control software, the experimental code is sent to the upgrade server for inspection and compilation. The checked and compiled code is then sent to the devices via a secured channel.

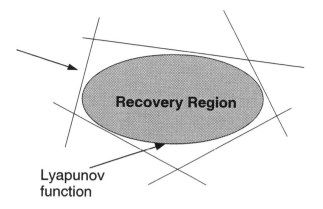

FIG. 3.1. *State constraints and the switching rule (Lyapunov function).*

Telelab's device level architecture is known as the Simplex architecture [14, 15], which is a dynamic real-time architecture that supports the online replacement of control software modules without interrupting the control operations.

The experimental controller is the one that is submitted by the user and may contain bugs and viruses. The baseline controller provides the normal control when there is either no experimental controller to run or the experimental controller fails. The safety controller is a specially designed robust controller that has a large stability envelope at the cost of control performance. It is used to stabilize the device after the experimental controller fails.

The decision module is the central part of the architecture. It evaluates the performance of the physical system and selects a control command from the controllers at each sampling period. Although all three controllers may be running, generating commands simultaneously, only one of the commands will be chosen to be sent to the physical system. The controller whose command is used to control the physical system is called active controller. The I/O module reads the measurements from the physical system and distributes them to all other modules, and receives the control command from the decision module and sends it to the physical system. The user interface module gets commands from the user and processes them, initializes the replacement unit management, and manages the processes. Figure 2.3 shows the complete basic structure of the Simplex architecture with the arrows indicating the directions of data flow.

The Simplex architecture is usually configured in two parts, a high assurance kernel and the application controllers. The former consists of the user interface, I/O module, decision module and a safety controller, while the latter includes a baseline controller and an experimental controller. The high assurance kernel is engineered to be highly reliable and its modules are not replaceable online. The application controllers, on the other hand, provide the chance to improve the system performance online, and they are implemented as replaceable units.

3. Semantic Faults and Service Availability. Other than obviously wrong outputs such as out of range control command, it is very difficult to determine if a controller's instantaneous output is correct. Some of the incorrect outputs from a faulty experimental controller will inevitably be sent to the device. We need to ensure that the device under control will remain in an admissible state, in spite of faulty control commands.

In the operation of a plant (or a vehicle), there is a set of state constraints, called operation constraints, representing the safety, device's physical limitations, environmental and other operation requirements. States that satisfy all these constraints are called admissible states. The operation constraints can be represented as a normalized polytope, $C^T X \leq 1$, in the N-dimensional state space of the system under control. Each line on the boundary represents a constraint, for example, the rotation of the engine must be no greater than K RPM.

To limit the loss that can be caused by a faulty controller, we must ensure that the system states are always admissible. That is, we must be able to 1) take the control away from a faulty controller and give it to a predefined safety controller before the system state becomes inadmissible, 2) the system is controllable by the safety controller after the switch, and 3) the future trajectory of the system state after the switch will stay within the set of admissible states. Note that we cannot use the boundary of the polytope as the switching rule, just as we cannot stop the car from collision, when the car is about to touch the wall. Physical systems have inertia.

A subset of the admissible states that satisfies these three conditions is called a recovery region. The recovery region is represented by a Lyapunov function inside the state constraint polytope. That is, the recovery region is a stability region within the state constraint polytope. Geometrically, a Lyapunov function defines an N-dimensional ellipsoid in the N-dimensional system state space as illustrated in Figure 3.1. As long as the system state is inside the ellipsoid associated with a controller, the system states under the given controller will stay within the ellipsoid and converge to the equilibrium position. Thus, we can use the boundary of the ellipsoid associated with the safety controller as the switching rule.

Lyapunov function is not unique for a given system and controller combination. In order not to unduly restrict the state space that can be used for control experiment, we need to find the largest ellipsoid within the polytope that represents the operational constraints. Mathematically, finding the largest ellipsoid inside a polytope can now be solved by the Linear Matrix Inequality (LMI) method [18]. Thus, we can use Lyapunov theory and the LMI tools to solve our recovery region problem. For example, giving a dynamic system $X' = A^* X + BKX$, where X is the system state, A^* is the system equation and K represents a controller. We can first choose K by using well understood controller designs with a robust stability, i.e., the system stability region is insensitive to model uncertainty.

The system under the control of this reliable controller is $X' = AX$, where

$A = (A^* + BK)$, where the stability condition is represented by $A^T Q + QA < 0$, and Q is the Lyapunov function. The operational constraints are represented by a normalized polytope, $C^T X \leq 1$. The largest ellipsoid inside the polytope can be found by minimizing $(log\ detQ^{-1})$, subject to stability condition. The resulting Q defines the largest normalized ellipsoid $X^T QX = 1$, the recovery region, inside the polytope as shown in Figure 3.1.

During run-time, the plant is normally under the control of the high performance control subsystem. The plant state X is being checked at every sampling period if it is within the N-dimensional ellipsoid by a simple test: if $X^T QX < k$, where k is a constant less than 1. $(1 - k)$ is the error margin to accommodate errors such as those in system state measurement. If $X^T QX \geq k$, the high assurance control subsystem takes over. This ensures that the operation of the plant never violates the operational constraints. It is important to note that the high assurance controller is a simple and well-understood classical controller. It is executing in parallel to the high performance controller and thus it is ready to take over at any time.

4. Capability Management Using Static Program Analysis.

4.1. Problem Definition. Even though the Simplex-based dynamic upgrade platform has restricted features compared to general purpose systems, all the aspects of the security problems should be considered to obtain the maximum security: confidentiality, integrity, and service availability. Among those areas, we focus on the integrity problem in this paper. Traditionally, resource protection and capability management techniques have been proposed as solutions to the integrity problems for general purpose computing environment. These solutions are to isolate each entity (i.e., a process or a task) by providing it with its own resource space so that the entity does not access outside the space without legitimate permissions. In order to access outside the private space, a capability for the access must be obtained. The capability is a pair consisting of a system resource id and the allowed permissions to access the resource.

Such solutions have been mainly provided by operating systems [5, 17, 19]. Complexity in managing the capabilities at run-time is of major concern for these approaches; the complexities vary depending on the granularity of the units where the capability or protection is enforced. One of the most coarse grain protection mechanisms provided by operating systems is the UNIX process mechanism. The UNIX process mechanism achieves the isolation of each process by the nature of UNIX memory management system cooperated with hardware memory management units. More sophisticated mechanisms provide finer grain capability management framework [17, 19] and uniform interface to manage various system resources. As the systems are connected to each other via the Internet and the mobility of software components drastically grows, such sophisticated techniques would be accepted in desktop and server platforms in spite of their complexities. However, in embedded real-time systems with limited system resources, the run-time overhead for the security checking should be minimized or avoided if possible. One objective of this paper is to introduce a security check

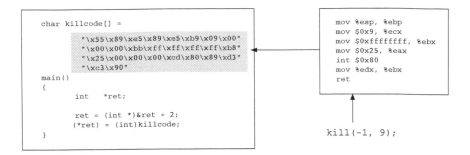

FIG. 4.1. *A stack smashing attack example*

technique that can detect the security vulnerabilities with as little run-time overhead as possible. We first characterize the security problems in the aspect of
integrity in the Simplex-based dynamic upgrade environment. This characteri-
zation will also be applicable to other embedded real-time systems using small
devices.

Any viable solution to the integrity problem must address three aspects:
resource management, process management, and *permission management*. The
resource management is to control the resource allocation for processes under certain system-wide resource allocation criteria. Examples of the resources whose
allocation should be managed at system-wide fashion include the memory. The
process management is to control the creation and deletion of processes (e.g.,
process creation by **fork** system call in UNIX systems). The permission management is to check whether a process is performing legitimate operations (read,
write, and execution) to a given resource.

We do not allow user control codes to dynamically allocate memory or manage process because these capabilities are not only unnecessary in control applications, but also making the system vulnerable to attacks[1]. That is, we
follow the principle of "least privilege". In modern hardware, since the user
codes are executed at user's state, to acquire the resource and process management capability, user codes must make system calls explicitly or implicitly.
The implicit calls are sequences of machine instructions implementing system
calls. Such instructions can be implemented directly as inline assembly codes,
hidden in unchecked external libraries or in data areas that will be executed
through pointer manipulations and jumps, or smashing through memory object
boundaries (e.g., stack smashing). Therefore, we should prevent using all kinds
of implicit calls as well as explicit system calls to obtain the maximum security.

Among these types of capability abuses, using explicit system calls, inserting
inline assembly statements, and using unchecked libraries are easily prevented.
On the other hand, preventing the execution of codes from data areas and the ac-

---

[1]In other applications, we will relax this restriction. But this is beyond the scope of this
paper.

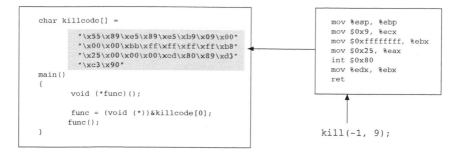

```
char killcode[] =

    "\x55\x89\xe5\x89\xe5\xb9\x09\x00"
    "\x00\x00\xbb\xff\xff\xff\xff\xb8"
    "\x25\x00\x00\xcd\x80\x89\xd3"
    "\xc3\x90"
main()
{
        void (*func)();

        func = (void (*))&killcode[0];
        func();
}
```

```
mov %esp, %ebp
mov $0x9, %ecx
mov $0xffffffff, %ebx
mov $0x25, %eax
int $0x80
mov %edx, %ebx
ret
```

```
kill(-1, 9);
```

FIG. 4.2. *A code execution from data area example*

cessing beyond memory object boundaries are not trivial. This is because of the unsafe nature of the C programming language. Most prevailing security attacks have been buffer overflow attacks that exploit the fact that the C programming language does not enforce any run-time type checking [3, 6, 7, 20]. This also holds for our platform since we assume that new control software components are submitted as C source codes.

Figure 4.1 and Figure 4.2 show two cases that prohibited system calls are invoked exploiting the unsafe features of the C programming language. (These examples assume that the underlying operating system has similar interfaces to those of UNIX.) Figure 4.1 uses the stack smashing attack so that the kill system call is called when returning from the main function. In the example, the last assignment statement modifies the memory contents outside the permitted stack area since the pointer ret points to outside the stack area due to the assignment at the second statement. The array, killcode, contains a sequence of machine codes to implicitly call kill system call terminating all the processes included in the same process group. Figure 4.2 uses a function pointer to execute codes stored in data area. The code also invokes the kill system call given as a sequence of machine codes contained in a data array. As shown in the figures, posing restrictions on system accesses at source code level does not guarantee preventing malicious use of system accesses if we use the C programming language.

In order to prevent the undesirable system accesses, we must ensure that *every memory access performs only the permitted operations (i.e., operations among read, write, and execution) to the area being accessed.* In particular, we should not allow write/modify operations across the permitted memory space boundaries such as arrays and stacks, in order to prevent the stack smashing attacks. In addition, we should not allow any execution of codes from data area, which allows malicious users to embed their code and execute it. Furthermore, such prevention should not incur significant run-time overhead in embedded real-time systems. In this paper, we propose a light-weight capability management technique based on a static program analysis method. We call this light-weight capability management *a memory object-based capability management.* The description on the exact meaning of the memory object and the method we adapted for the static capability management is given in the following section.

4.2. Security Check Using Static Program Analysis. We consider memory space as the major resource to be protected in this paper while any system resource can be target of the protection. In this section, the unit for the static capability management is defined and the proposed capability management method is described.

4.2.1. Memory Object and Capability. A memory object, an address range of system memory space, is the unit where the permissions on the operations are assigned. The operations consist of read (r), write (w), and execution (x): The r permission allows reading the contents from the corresponding memory object. The w permission allows erasing or modifying the contents of the corresponding memory object. The x permission allows code execution from the memory object. Each memory object has the unique identifier. A capability is a pair made up of this unique memory object identifier and a set of permitted operations on that memory object. For each process, a set of capabilities is required during its execution depending on the amount of memory space the process will use for various purposes.

The rules of creating memory objects are as follows:

- Every static data variable creates a memory object. We call this kind of object *data object*. A data object has two attributes, the symbol name (i.e., start address) and the size of the variable.
- All the local variables create a single memory object. We call this kind of object *stack object*. A stack object has the size of the stack frame as its attribute.
- Every code label creates a memory object. We call this kind of object *label object*. The size of a label object is not defined.
- Every function name creates a memory object. We call this object *function object*. We do not consider the size of the function object in this paper while the size of each function can be determined statically. Further restriction on the function object posed in this paper is that we do not allow any function calls to external functions except the *trusted functions*. The possibility of the extension of our framework by removing these restrictions is discussed in Section 6.

For each memory object created, a set of permissions is given to form a capability. The rules of the capability formation by the compiler are as follows:

- Each data object and stack object is given r and w permissions.
- Each label object and function object is given r and x permissions.

Consider Figure 4.1 and Figure 4.2 as examples to see how we can create the capabilities and how the attacks using stack smashing and code execution from data area are detected using the capability information. In Figure 4.1, a function object (i.e., main function), a data object (i.e., array killcode), and a stack object are created. Since the size of the stack object is determined as the size of an integer variable (i.e., 4 bytes), the last statement of the main function is detected as an illegal operation and the compiler generates a security alarm. Moreover, since return address of the `main` function is modified to the address of the array `killcode`, another alarm will be generated due to the code execution from the data object. In Figure 4.2, a security alarm at the last statement in function `main` will be generated due to the code execution from the data area. In the following subsection, the explanation on how we can generate the security alarms at compile time is given.

4.2.2. Static Program Analysis. The objective of our static security check is to detect all the capability violations before run-time. In order to identify whether a memory access violates given capabilities or not, the exact address (or the offset from the start address of the corresponding memory object) of the memory access should be known. One method to get the exact addresses of all the memory accesses before run-time is to simulate the execution of the program providing all the possible inputs to the program. However, this method cannot be performed because finding all the possible inputs is not feasible and such extensive simulation will cause tremendous overhead. Static security check techniques without tracking all the execution paths of programs have been proposed by a number of research groups [2, 13, 21, 27, 20]. The techniques use simple static analysis method to induce the range of the address of each memory access. However, the accuracy of the techniques is not acceptable to our objectives due to their methods' limitations. Moreover, the techniques focus on the bounds checking of arrays without provision for generic capability violation detection. Other techniques include compile time code instrumentation method to check buffer-overflows at run-time such as Stackguard [6, 7] and Bounds Checking GCC [8]. Proof-Carrying Code [11] is a technique that a proof on the safety of codes is included in the executable binary so that the underlying operating system can check the safety of the codes based on the proof. One drawback of the approach is that the proof should be generated manually at the development phase.

Considering both the complexity of the security check and the accuracy of the results, we adapted a symbolic execution method with an intermediate level complexity between the extensive simulation method and the existing static methods. Our technique combines two static program analysis techniques: a static execution time analysis technique originally proposed by Lundqvist et al. [10] to traverse the execution flow of programs and a static analysis for data caching proposed by White et al. [22] to extract the address representation for each memory access.

Program Representation. We assume that each C source code is converted to a register transfer language (RTL) form or an assembly language of a RISC machine. Examples of the RTL forms include the RTL form of the GNU CC and the intermediate representation form of the Zephyr package [12]. Since the RTL forms emulate RISC style virtual machines, their semantics are similar to those of the assembly languages of real RISC machines. Figure 4.3 shows an example of the RTL form. Figure 4.3(b) and Figure 4.3(c) represent the RTL

FIG. 4.3. *Intermediate representation*

forms for the C code in Figure 4.3(a) that is reused from Figure 4.1. Among the RTL forms, the RTL form in Figure 4.3(c) is an expanded form of the RTL form in Figure 4.3(b) to make detection of capability violations easy.

Our compiler's RTL form is based on that of GNU CC. In the RTL form, r[x] represents Register x; the registers are assumed to be virtual registers in this RTL form. M[reg] shows the memory address indicated by the contents of the *reg*. *reg* can be a register or an expression including registers. If the M[reg] is used at the left side, it represents the memory address and the RTL statement shows a store operation. On the other hand, if the M[reg] is used at the right side, it represents the contents of the address and the RTL statement represents a load operation. We will use the simple RTL form throughout this paper.

Each register holds either an exact value or *unknown*. At the beginning of a program, every register has unknown as its value. During the symbolic execution, the values of some of the registers are modified to exact values. The exact values include integer constants and the addresses of memory objects. The unknown values propagate to other registers or memory locations by arithmetic, logical, and load/store operations. For example, in an arithmetic operation, r[3]=r[1]+r[2], once either r[1] or r[2] has unknown value, then the value of r[3] changes to unknown. This also holds for load/store operations. For example, in a load operation r[2]=M[r[1]], if the value of r[1] is *unknown*, the value of r[2] becomes unknown.

To achieve the objective of our static analysis, we concentrate on the representation of each memory address. Concerning the representation of memory locations or memory object, we make the following definitions or restrictions:

- Before the content of a data object for an array is accessed, the start address of the data object is assigned to a register. We call this register *the base register* for the data object corresponding to the array.
- Every access to local variables is represented as the form, 'sp-*offset*', where sp is the stack pointer. In this paper, we do not consider the case that the local variables are allocated to registers.
- Every memory address should be represented by an expression made up of registers and constants; the expression must have only one base register including the stack pointer. In other words, the expression should be represented as 'r[x]+ *exp*' or '(sp-*offset*) + *exp*' where *exp* can be combination of registers whose values are unknown and constants. This

poses a limitation on programming syntax that can be accommodated by our framework. However, this limitation is acceptable for mission critical or real-time applications since these applications usually do not utilize complex syntax. The effect of loosening this restriction is included in our future research subject.

In the example Figure 4.3, two memory accesses for write operations, one at the second RTL statement and the other at the last RTL statement, should be carefully investigated to identify whether the memory accesses violate given capabilities. As shown in the expanded RTL form in Figure 4.3(c), the memory access in the second RTL statement is legal since its access is within the legitimate area of the stack object for the variable ret. However, the memory access in the last RTL statement is illegal since it accesses the location 4 bytes away from the stack pointer. In the following section, the program analysis steps for the symbolic execution and the issues in considering multiple execution paths in a program are explained.

Analysis Steps. In our framework, analyzing a program using the symbolic execution method follows three steps: *memory object creation step, control flow analysis step*, and RTL *expansion step*. At the memory object creation step, all the memory objects are created based on the memory object creation rules described in Section 4.1. At the control flow analysis step, a control flow graph is built based on the RTL representation or the assembly instruction sequences generated by the compiler. At the RTL expansion step, the base registers are identified and the address for each memory access is represented by an expression using a base register. Whether given capabilities are violated is checked in statement-by-statement manner, traversing the control flow graph. During the traversing, the loops are effectively unrolled to check the memory accesses included in the loops accurately.

Execution Path Analysis. Conditional statements generate multiple execution paths in a program. One advantage of using the symbolic execution is in handling the conditional statements. By the symbolic execution, the values of variables are traced as accurately as possible during the execution, although the values for some variables are unknown. This gives a chance to exclude an execution path from the paths to be considered in the security check. We can exclude a path when the exact value of a conditional statement is identified and the value reveals that one of the paths from the conditional statement is not feasible. Once a variable for condition check has an exact value at the time of analyzing the statement, the control flow following the statement would be determined according to the condition check. For example, for a conditional statement that has an RTL form, if (r[1]<x), once the values for r[1] and x are all determined as exact values, the control flow following this statement is determined statically. On the other hand, if the value of the variable is unknown, both of the two execution paths following the statement should be considered. However a problem of execution path explosion arises if a program has a sequence of conditional statements or a loop with conditional statements in the body.

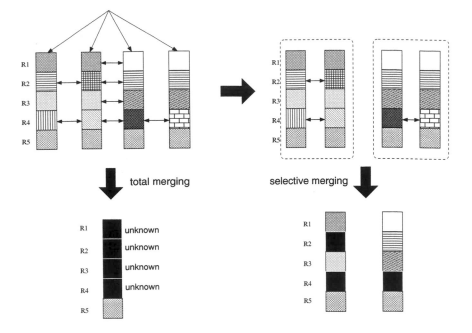

FIG. 4.4. *Path merging method.*

The execution path explosion is handled by introducing a path merging method that is originally proposed by Lundqvist et al. [10]. The path merging is to merge several execution paths into a single path information combining the values of registers from different execution paths. Originally, the path merging is performed at each iteration in a loop with more than one execution path in the body. For example, if two different execution paths assign a register two different values, merging the two paths results in assigning *unknown* value to the register. Therefore, path merging might lead to inaccurate analysis results while keeping the analysis complexity controllable.

In order to avoid the significant loss of accuracy during merging, we can defer the path merging until certain threshold is reached in terms of the number of paths maintained. When the merging becomes inevitable due to the complexity threshold, we apply a *selective path merging* instead of merging all the paths into a single one (*total merging*). The selective path merging is to carefully merge the execution paths so that the loss of the accuracy can be minimized. The path merging in our technique works as follows: First, we should identify for each pair of execution paths that how many registers are assigned different values. The execution path pairs with the least number of different register assignments are candidate for path merging. Second, after the merging execution paths selected from the first stage, we continue the path selection and merging if further reduction of the number of execution paths is required due to a certain

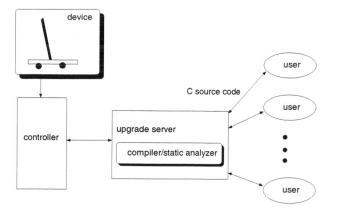

FIG. 5.1. *Dynamic upgrade platform.*

threshold on the number of execution paths to be maintained. By applying the selective merging, we can minimize the accuracy loss while effectively reducing the number of paths to be tracked down.

Figure 4.4 illustrates the total merging and selective merging methods. Since the four execution paths assign different values to the four (R1, R2, R3, and R4) out of the five registers, the registers are assigned *unknown* values after the total merging. However, if we choose carefully the paths to be merged as shown in the selective merging part of the figure, the number of registers to be assigned unknown values is decreased to two as shown in the selective merging part in the figure while the selective merging should maintain one more execution path than the total merging afterwards.

5. Implementation.

5.1. Design. Figure 5.1 shows the overall platform design of the Telelab environment enhanced with the proposed static security check framework. In the environment, the inverted pendulum equipped with optical encoders is controlled by an embedded computer under the supervision of a slimmed-down version of the Simplex. The static security check is done on a separate computer, the upgrade server, which also accepts the submissions of control codes from users. The controller network is isolated from users in that the communication link between the upgrade server and controller is a dedicated line and not connected to publicly accessible network.

The Linux-based upgrade server has a web-based interface for accepting source codes from users. As illustrated in Figure 5.1, once a piece of source code written in the restricted syntax is submitted, it is being fed to the static security check tools including a modified version of a compiler. If the code passes the check, the library for the Simplex API is linked to produce a readily executable binary for the embedded computer. The API provides the user code with a way to communicate with the core of the Simplex, namely, querying the device status and reporting the control commands. Over the dedicated channel, the generated binary is then transferred to the embedded computer, the target platform, which controls the inverted pendulum.

As a part of the slimmed-down Simplex, the embedded computer also has an interface through which it accepts executable binaries from the upgrade server. This interface is equivalent to the user interface module of the Simplex in Figure 2.3, as it is also used to manage the embedded computer by querying the device status or manually switching the active controller. Through the Simplex API, the interface is also closely linked to the core Simplex modules, which include the decision module, I/O module and safety module, similarly to the previous versions of the Simplex but only in a much compact form, making it suitable for embedded applications. Up on reception of the binary, the interface passes the submitted binary to the user-space helper application, which executes it. The newly started control software then contacts the Simplex core to receive the sensor readings and to report the control command it produces. If the reported control command fails the safety check described in Section 4, the user controller module is killed and the internal safety controller becomes the active controller. Similarly in case of timing fault, the safety controller is promoted to the active controller and the user controller module is removed whenever it misses its deadline. In order to reduce the timing faults at run-time, a worst case execution time analysis technique can be applied before sending in the controller to the embedded computer.

The core of the Simplex is protected from any user space activity by the Linux operating systems' kernel protection, as it resides in the kernel space, exposing only the predefined interface via virtual devices. The core is also tightly bound to the timer interrupt service routine, making it possible to maintain stability of the inverted pendulum even under some cases of Linux kernel crash which do not corrupt the ISR and the data structures tied to it. Prevention of any system resource abuse, including accessing other processes' private memory space is enforced by the static security check in compilation time.

The upgrade server has the compilation systems augmented with the proposed static check technique. The three steps, memory object creation, control flow analysis, and RTL expansion steps, are implemented inside an existing compiler and coordinate with the front-end stage of the compiler to get the information on the variable definitions. After the static check is performed, the compiler generates security alarms if needed and the doubtful application is not sent to the embedded computer. Once the application passes the security check by the compiler, the linking is performed using the Simplex API library to generate the executable form of the application.

5.2. Proof-of-Concept Implementation. In order to demonstrate the feasibility of the proposed security check framework, we implemented a proof-of-concept platform. For the control system part, the Simplex is implemented onto the AM5x86-133 (i486 compatible) based single board computer (SBC) equipped with an AD/DA converter. We modified the Linux operating system to

TABLE 5.1
Benchmark programs

program	description
FFT	performs FFT on 1024 complex array.
LMSFIR	performs 32-tap LMS adaptive FIR filter processing on 64 points.
MULT	performs $[10 \times 10]$ $\times [10 \times 10]$ matrix multiplication.
IIR	performs 4-cascaded IIR biquad filter processing on 64 points.
COMPRESS	performs an image compression of a 128×128 pixel image by a factor of 4:1 using the DCT (discrete cosine transform).
EDGE_DETECT	performs edge detection on the edges in a 256 gray-level 128×128 pixel image.

be used in the platform; the interrupt handling (especially bottom half handling) is restricted to guarantee bounded execution times of the interrupts for real-time operation of control applications. The software components occupy about 2 MBytes of memory in total: the modified Linux kernel uses about 500 KBytes and the file system image occupies about 1.5 MBytes. The Simplex part in the system consumes only about 20 KBytes.

The static security check module is implemented in an existing GCC (version 2.95.2 configured for i686-pc-linux-gnu). Since the security check module is implemented at the RTL level of the GCC, the module can be potentially used regardless of the underlying hardware platforms. The security check is enabled by '-fsecurity-check' option.

The control software running on the platform to control the inverted pendulum is a conventional feedback controller that gets input data from sensors and computes control law to be used as the next input to the controlled device. We conducted a number of experiments using the control software by inserting hacking codes. The hacking codes based on buffer overflow attacks or capability abuse (i.e., code execution from the data area) attacks were successfully detected by the security enhanced compilation system in the upgrade server.

In order to validate the applicability of the proposed technique to various real-time applications, we performed an analysis on the memory reference behaviors of control and DSP applications. We used the UTDSP (University of Toronto DSP) Benchmark Suite [26] for the validation purpose. The UTDSP Benchmark Suite was created to evaluate the quality of code generated by a high-level language (such as C) compiler targeting a programmable digital signal processor (DSP).

The programs chosen from the UTDSP Benchmark Suite are shown in Table 5.1. We performed an analysis on the benchmark programs to investigate the properties of the programs. One notable observation is that the addresses of all the memory references for write operations can be identified statically due to the simple structures of the programs. This implies that most of the memory addresses of the chosen programs can be easily calculated using a number of statically traceable values such as the values of loop induction variables. Moreover, the memory addresses are mostly determined regardless of the preceding execution paths taken, which implies that the impact of the inaccuracy by merging execution paths in our framework could be very small. The observations reveal the applicability of the proposed static program analysis for security check to the special domain applications including control and real-time applications.

6. Conclusion and Future Work. Although the peacetime behavior of this new architecture is almost identical to the previous version of Telelab, the addition of the static security check and the slimmed-down Simplex makes it more secure and practical. In the previous version, Telelab's compilation server did not have ability to check the integrity of the submitted code, exposing the system to well-known security related attacks. By introducing compilation time static check combined with the restricted C language syntax which reduces the possibility of abusing the power of the language, we were able to overcome the three vulnerability elements, timing faults, semantic faults, and capability abuse. For control applications the restricted programming language syntax poses very little restrictions on the language's programmability and applicability. In addition, the compilation time static check minimizes the run-time overhead of capability management, which is desirable in the context of embedded applications. Furthermore, the employment of the slimmed-down Simplex also minimizes the overhead of detecting run-time timing and semantic faults, making the control system safe and more light-weighted. These synergic benefits make a Simplex-based dynamic upgrade environment more practical and secure without incurring heavy run-time penalty.

In the future, we will extend the applicability of this framework to a broader range of applications beyond the control systems. This broadening of application range necessitates the relaxation of the restrictions posed in the current framework. For example, the system calls should be used in user applications to utilize system facilities. Applying the proposed static check technique to such applications may generate a bunch of false alarms since the compiler will determine conservatively when it cannot exactly identify whether the system calls are safely used or not. As the features that are used by applications increase and their usage become more sophisticated, the effect of the conservative decision by the compiler will become significant.

One possible solution is to provide a framework for tight interaction between the compiler and the underlying operating system. At the operating system's side, an extensive knowledge of its facilities including system calls should be given to the compiler so that the compiler can use during the static security check phase. On the other hand, the results of the static security check by the compiler should be given to the operating system so that the operating system can utilize its own protection mechanism (e.g., a fine grain capability management) to cover the vulnerabilities that are not detected at compile time. Even under the interaction, the compiler's role should be maximized to minimize the run-time cost of the security checks; the operating system support for the resource protection and capability management should be a light-weight implementation. Using the compiler-operating system cooperation, broader range of applications can be accommodated in the system without making any compromise in system security. Our future research will focus on the compiler-operating system cooperation for the system security.

Acknowledgments. This work is sponsored in part by the Office of Naval Research, in part by Seoul National University under Brain Korea 21 which supports Sung-Soo Lim's work at UIUC. We also want to thank Prof. Sang Lyul Min at Seoul National University for his encouragement on Sung-Soo Lim's work. Finally, we want to thank Prasanna Krishnan for her reviews and comments.

REFERENCES

[1] M. AMIN. Towards Self-Healing Infrastructure Systems. *IEEE Computer*, pages 44–52, Aug. 2000.

[2] T. M. AUSTIN, S. E. BREACH, AND G. S. SOHI. Efficient Detection of All Pointer and Array Access Errors. In *Proceedings of the SIGPLAN 1994 Conference on Programming Languages Design and Implementation*, June 1994.

[3] A. BARATLOO, T. TSAI, AND N. SINGH. Transparent Run-Time Defense Against Stack Smashing Attacks. In *Proceedings of the USENIX Annual Technical Conference*, June 2000.

[4] G. BORRIELLO AND R. WAN. Embedded Computation Meets the World Wide Web. *Communications of the ACM*, pages 59–66, May 2000.

[5] J. S. CHASE, H. M. LEVY, M. J. FEELEY, AND E. D. LAZOWSKA. Sharing and Protection in a Single Address-Space Operating Systems. *ACM Transactions on Computer Systems*, 12(4):271–307, Nov. 1994.

[6] C. COWAN, C. PU, D. MAIER, H. HINTON, J. WALPOLE, P. BAKKE, S. BEATTIE, A. GRIER, P. WAGLE, AND Q. ZHANG. Stackguard: Automatic Adaptive Detection and Prevention of Buffer-Overflow Attacks. In *Proceedings of the 7th USENIX Security Symposium*, pages 63–78, Jan. 1998.

[7] C. COWAN, P. WAGLE, C. PU, S. BEATTIE, AND J. WALPOLE. Buffer Overflows: Attacks and Defenses for the Vulnerability of the Decade. In *DARPA Information Survivability Conference and Exposition*, Jan. 2000.

[8] R. W. M. JONES AND P. H. J. KELLY. Backwards-Compatible Bounds Checking for Arrays and Pointers in C Programs. In *Proceedings of the Third International Workshop on Automated Debugging*, 1997.

[9] H. KIM. Analysis of Data Cache References Based on Abstract Interpretation. Master's thesis, Seoul National University, 1999.

[10] T. LUNDQVIST AND P. STENSTRÖM. Integrating Path and Timing Analysis Using Instruction-Level Simulation Techniques. In *Proceedings of 1998 ACM SIGPLAN Workshop on Languages, Compilers, and Tools for Embedded Systems*, June 1998.

[11] G. C. NECULA. Proof Carrying Code. In *Proceedings of the 1997 Symposium on Principles of Programming Languages (POPL97)*, Jan. 1997.

[12] N. RAMSEY AND J. W. DAVIDSON. Machine Descriptions to Build Tools for Embedded Systems. In *Proceedings of the ACM SIGPLAN 1998 Workshop on Languages,*

Compilers, and Tools for Embedded Systems, June 1998.

[13] R. RUGINA AND M. RINARD. Symbolic Bounds Analysis of Pointers, Array Indices, and Accessed Memory Regions. In *Proceedings of the SIGPLAN'2000 Conference on Programming Language Design and Implementation*, pages 182–195, June 2000.

[14] D. SETO, B. H. KROGH, AND L. SHA. Dynamic Control System Upgrade Using the Simplex Architecture. *IEEE Control Systems Magazine*, 18(4):72–80, Aug. 1998.

[15] L. SHA. Dependable System Upgrade. In *Proceedings of the 19th Real-Time Systems Symposium*, pages 440–448, 1998.

[16] L. SHA, R. RAJKUMAR, AND S. SATHAYE. Generalized Rate Monotonic Scheduling Theory: A Framework of Developing Real-Time Systems. *IEEE Proceedings*, Jan. 1994.

[17] J. S. SHAPIRO, J. M. SMITH, AND D. J. FARBER. EROS: A Fast Capability System. *Operating Systems Review*, 34(5):170–185, Dec. 1999.

[18] L. VANDENBERGHE, S. BOYD, AND S.-P. WU. Determinant Maximization with Linear Matrix Inequality Constraints. *SIAM Journal on Matrix Analysis and Applications*, 19, 1998.

[19] J. VOCHTELLO, S. RUSSEL, AND G. HEISER. Capability-based Protection in the Mungi Operating System. In *Proceedings of the 3rd International Workshop on Object Orientation in Operating Systems*, pages 108–115, 1993.

[20] D. A. WAGNER. *Static Analysis and Computer Security: New Techniques for Software Assurance*. PhD thesis, University of California at Berkeley, 2000.

[21] D. A. WAGNER, J. FOSTER, E. BREWER, AND A. AIKEN. A First Step Towards Automated Detection of Buffer Overrun Vulnerabilities. In *Network and Distributed System Security Symposium*, Feb. 2000.

[22] R. WHITE, F. MUELLER, C.HEALY, D. WHALLEY, AND M. HARMON. Timing Analysis for Data Caches and Set-Associative Caches. In *Proceedings of the 3rd IEEE Real-Time Technology and Applications Symposium*, pages 192–202, 1997.

[23] DARPA News Releases.
http://www.darpa.mil/body/newsre.html.

[24] Telelab project at University of Illinois at Urbana-Champaign.
http://www-drii.cs.uiuc.edu/project.html.

[25] Controls Web Lab, University of Illinois at Urbana-Champaign.
http://weblab.ge.uiuc.edu.

[26] UTDSP Benchmark Suite.
http://www.eecg.toronto.edu/ conrinna/DSP/infrastructure/UTDSP.html.

[27] Z. XU, B. P. MILLER, AND T. REPS. Safety Checking of Machine Code. In *Proceedings of the SIGPLAN 2000 Conference on Programming Language Design and Implementation (PLDI'2000)*, June 2000.

DECISION TREE CLASSIFIERS FOR COMPUTER INTRUSION DETECTION

XIANGYANG LI AND NONG YE *

Abstract. Intrusion detection is required to protect the security of computer network systems by detecting intrusive activities occurring in computer network systems. In this paper, we present decision tree techniques that are used to automatically learn intrusion signatures and classify activities in computer network systems as normal or intrusive for intrusion detection. We show the design of decision tree classifiers for intrusion detection, using different features of raw activity data in computer network systems and different sizes of observation windows. The performance of decision tree classifiers is discussed. We also present the impact of noises in data on the detection performance of the decision tree classifiers. Computer audit data from the Basic Security Module of the Solaris operating system are used to train and test the decision tree classifiers.

Key words. computer security, intrusion detection, signature recognition, data mining, and decision tree

1. Introduction. With the rapid development and application of computing and communication technologies, computer network security has become increasingly critical to protect computer network systems from intrusions. An intrusion is a series of activities in a computer network system that compromise security of the system [1]. An intrusion may be an external attack or an internal misuse. An intrusion may compromise availability, integrity, confidentiality and/or other security aspects of a computer network system in many different ways [2]-[5].

Intrusion detection signals intrusive activities occurring in computer network systems. It is essential in protecting computer network systems from intrusions, either internal or external, as intrusion prevention mechanisms (e.g., firewall, encryption and authentication) cannot completely prevent intrusions from breaking into computer network systems. Many intrusion detection systems have been developed [6], [7]. The core of an intrusion detection system is an analysis engine that analyzes data of activities observed in computer network systems to detect intrusive activities. Intrusion detection systems have used data analysis algorithms from a variety of fields such as statistics, data mining, and machine learning. Some examples of the data analysis algorithms are the state transition analysis, Petri net, rule-based expert systems, association rules, neural networks, statistical analysis, Bayesian networks, computer immunology, and genetic algorithms [8]-[15]. Some comparisons of system performance can be found in [16], [17].

Existing intrusion detection systems focus on two kinds of activity data from a computer network system: network traffic data and computer audit data. Network traffic data contain data packets communicated between host machines to

---

*Department of Industrial Engineering , P.O. Box 875906, Arizona State University, Tempe, Arizona, 85287-5906 (xyli@ieee.org, nongye@asu.edu).

capture activities over network links. Computer audit data capture activities occurring on individual host machines. There are often huge amounts of activity data. Data from a computer network system can easily contain hundreds of thousands of network connection records or computer audit records per day. A data field in a data record presents an attribute of activities, and may take the form of a nominal variable such as event type, user ID, process ID, command name, remote IP (Internet Protocol) address, or a numerical variable such as a time stamp of event, CPU time, etc. Intrusive activities usually occur while normal activities are ongoing in computer network systems. Hence, collected activity data have a mixture of normal activities and intrusive activities. If we consider normal activities as "white noises" and intrusive activities as "signals" that we want to detect, then noises exist in activity data collected from a computer network system.

Data analysis for intrusion detection has taken mainly two approaches: anomaly detection, and signature recognition (pattern matching) [19], [20]. Anomaly detection techniques learn the normal behavior of a subject in a computer network system and build the norm profile. The subject may be a user, a host machine or a network. Using the norm profile, anomaly detection techniques look for intrusive activities that deviate largely from the norm profile. Signature recognition techniques learn signatures of intrusive activities manually or automatically from historic data of intrusive and normal activities. Signature recognition techniques match these signatures against data of observed activities in a computer network system to determine the intrusiveness of the activities.

Anomaly detection techniques can detect both unknown and known intrusions if they demonstrate large deviations from the norm profile. However, anomaly detection techniques may produce false alarms if anomalies are caused by behavioral irregularities instead of intrusions. Signature recognition is accurate at detecting known intrusions if their signatures have been learned, but cannot detect novel intrusions whose signatures are unknown. Hence, both anomaly detection techniques and signature recognition techniques are necessary, and should be used together to complement each other. This paper focuses on signature recognition techniques.

Intrusion signatures can be manually learned and coded into intrusion detection systems by human experts [19]. However, it is tedious for human experts to manually learn, code and update many intrusion signatures into an intrusion detection system. Commercial intrusion detection systems have relied mostly on manual coding and updating of intrusion signatures. Research prototype systems based on state-transition analysis and Petri net, also lack the capability of automatic learning and update.

Automatic learning of intrusion signatures from historic data of intrusive and normal activities offers the advantages in learning and updating intrusion signatures as more intrusion methods are noticed and data of these intrusion methods are collected. Association rule algorithms [13] have been used to learn intrusion signatures automatically from data. Association rule algorithms learn combinations of variable values that appear together in the same data record frequently and represent such combinations as rules of intrusion signatures. Take an example of two variables, X and Y, and each variable can take the value of 0, 1 or 2. If the combination of X=1 and Y=1 appears together in the same data record 99 times out of 100 data records for intrusive activities, then we form the following rule:

IF a data record has X=1 and Y=1 THEN signal this data record as intrusive.

This is a pattern of intrusion signature learned from association rule algorithms that recognize a highly frequent association of X=1 and Y=1.

An intrusion signature may be a high frequency of X=1 but with a low frequency of Y=2. That is, most times when X=1 appears in intrusive activities, Y=2 does not appear. Hence, this is a pattern of intrusion signature with a high frequency of X=1 together with a low frequency of Y=2 (Y taking the value of either 0 or 1 instead of 2), in other terms, X=1 and Y<=1. An intrusion signature may also be that X=0 never appears in intrusive activities. That is, X=0 has a low frequency in intrusive activities. Therefore, there are patterns of intrusion signature involving a low frequency of a variable value. In general, association rule algorithms cannot learn such patterns of intrusion signature. These algorithms are limited to the learning of only high frequency - high frequency associations but not associations involving low frequency.

We investigate decision tree algorithms that can learn a more comprehensive set of intrusion signature patterns for intrusion detection. This paper presents our study that uses decision tree algorithms to automatically learn and classify intrusion signatures. In [21], a simple application of the decision tree technique to intrusion detection is presented. Our study addresses issues in designing decision tree classifiers to detect intrusions, including the issue of extracting features from raw activity data, and the issue of performance impact of noises in data.

In the following sections, we first review the decision tree technique. Then we define the problem of intrusion detection for data sets with different levels of noises. We describe four different feature extraction methods that lead to different designs of the decision tree classifiers. Finally, the performance results of these different decision tree classifiers are compared and discussed.

2. Decision tree technique. There are two types of variables involved in the decision tree technique [22]-[25]: target variable, and predictor variable(s). The value of the target variable for a data record often indicates the class of this data record (called the target class). The values of predictor variables in a data record are used to predict the value of the target variable for this data record or classify this data record.

During training, the decision tree technique partitions examples of data records in the training data (called training examples) recursively until a stopping criterion is met. After each partition, the set of training examples falling in a branch of the decision tree has less inconsistency with respect to the target class. A typical stopping criterion for not further partitioning a branch is that all the examples are of the same target class, and the branch becomes a leaf in the decision tree.

The structure of a decision tree shows the relationship between the predictor variables and the target variable for a given problem. The decision tree divides the problem space into a number of sub-regions with all the training examples (data points) in one sub-region having the same target value. The sub-regions can then be used to classify the target value of new data. Each path from the root node of a decision tree to a leaf node of the decision tree represents a pattern of the predictor variables or a sub-region that is useful in predicting the value of the target variable.

Variables involved in the decision tree technique can be numerical or nominal. If a variable has numerical values, methods exist to find the split of continuous values into categorical values, thus transforming the variable into a nominal variable [22].

In this study, we use a commercial software package from SPCC Inc., AnswerTree 2.0, to build our decision trees. We use two of the four decision tree algorithms provided in AnswerTree 2.0: CHAID and GINI [26]. CHAID uses a chi-square test to find the most significant non-binary split points on the predictor variables. GINI is essentially CART [23]-[25] with the GINI index that produces binary trees. The GINI impurity index is defined as the possibility at a test node that a randomly chosen case is classified incorrectly. We choose CHAID to have an algorithm for non-binary trees and GINI to have an algorithm for binary trees.

3. Problem definition. In this section, we describe the activity data that are collected from a computer network system. We present four methods to extract features from raw activities data for detecting intrusions. Then we show the application of the decision tree technique to intrusion detection.

3.1. Training and testing data sets. The Basic Security Module (BSM) in the Solaris operating system can be used to audit activities on a host machine with the Solaris operating system. We use BSM audit data in this study. Audit data consist of audit records in sequence, one audit record for each audit event. Each audit record contains attributes of the audit event. Some examples of the attributes are event type, user ID, process ID, command name, event time, and remote IP address. In our study, we use only the information of event type, since many existing studies have shown the effectiveness of the event type information in intrusion detection [8]-[17]. There are 284 different event types in the Solaris operating system.

We use BSM audit data of normal activities from the MIT Lincoln Laboratory that creates these data by simulating normal activities on a host machine with the Solaris operating system. BSM audit data of intrusive activities are collected by simulating fifteen different intrusion scenarios in our laboratory on a host machine with the same version of the Solaris operating system. The audit data of normal activities contain 3019 audit events. The audit data of intrusive activities contain 1751 audit events.

For the application of the decision tree technique, we need training data of both intrusive and normal activities to create a decision tree that captures signature patterns of both intrusive and normal activities. Training data of both intrusive and normal activities are needed in order to discover signature patterns that are unique to intrusive activities. To test the detection performance of the decision tree technique, we need testing data of both intrusive and normal activities.

Hence, the audit data of 3019 events for normal activities are divided into approximately two halves. One half containing the first 1613 normal events is put into the training data set. Another half containing 1406 normal events is put into the testing data set. The audit data of the first eight intrusion scenarios containing 528 audit events are put into the training data set. The first part of the 1751 intrusive events, containing 528 audit events for the first eight of the fifteen intrusion scenarios, is put into the training data set. The remaining 1225 intrusive events are put into the testing data set. Hence, the training data set contains the 1613 normal events and the 526 intrusive events. The testing data set contains the 1406 normal events and the 1225 intrusive events. In the training and testing data sets, only 30 different event types appear. Hence, in the following text, we consider only 30 different event types instead of all the 284 possible event types.

To test performance impact of noises in data, we create two levels of noises in data: low and high. For the low noise level, the 1613 normal events and the 526 intrusive events in the training data set are arranged in two separate data blocks in sequence, and the 1406 normal events and the 1225 intrusive events in the testing data set are also arranged in two separate data blocks in sequence. Hence, for the low noise level, there is no mixture between the intrusion events and the normal events. The training data set contains an event stream of first the 1613 normal events and then the 526 intrusive events, and the testing data set contains an event stream of first the 1406 normal events and then the 1225 intrusive events.

In the real world, intrusive activities usually occur in a computer network system while there are also normal activities as background noises in the computer network system. The mixture of intrusive events with normal events is expected. For the high noise level, the 1613 normal events and the 526 intrusive events in the training data set are mixed in a random manner while maintaining the sequential order of all the normal events and the sequential order of all the intrusive events. This is accomplished by randomly selecting the next event in the event stream of the training data set from either the subset of the normal events or the subset of the intrusive events, until all the 1613 normal events and the 526 intrusive events have been selected into the event stream of the training data set. The testing data set is created in the same way for the high noise level. Table 3.1 shows three sets of training and testing data using different noise levels for the training data set and the testing data set: pure, mixed, and noisy. In the pure data sets, both the training data set and the testing data set have the low noise level. In the mixed data sets, the training data set has the low noise

Xiangyang Li and Nong Ye

TABLE 3.1
Pure, mixed, and noisy data sets.

	Pure	Mixed	Noisy
Training data set	low noise level	low noise level	high noise level
Testing data set	low noise level	high noise level	high noise level

level, and the testing data set has the high noise level. In the noisy data sets, both the training data set and the testing data set has the high noise level.

3.2. Problem representation. Whenever we observe a new event in a computer network system, we want to evaluate whether this event is normal or intrusive. A simple feature that we can extract from this event for intrusion detection is its event type. Hence, a simple feature extraction method is to use a predictor variable to represent the event type of this event. Since there are 30 different event types in our data sets, this predictor variable has 30 possible values. For each event in an event stream, we obtain a data record with the value of one predictor variable. This is a categorical value indicating the event type of the event. The target variable for this data record should indicate the target class of this event. There are two possible target classes: normal and intrusive. The value of the predictor variable is used to classify this event as normal or intrusive, that is, assign a target value to this data record. Hence, in this simple feature extraction method, the data record for each event has a predictor variable indicating the event type of this event and a target variable indicating the intrusiveness (normal or intrusive) of this event. If this event is an intrusive event, the target variable should have the target value of 1 (intrusive); otherwise the target variable should have the target value of 0 (normal). We call this feature extraction method the Single Event method. A decision tree built from a training data set using this feature extraction method is called a Single Event classifier.

Considering an event stream as time series data [27], we also develop three other feature extraction methods: Moving Window, EWMA Vector, and State-ID.

In the Moving Window method, we use an observation window to extract a feature of the event sequence in this observation window. As shown in Fig. 3.1, we move an observation window along an event stream. A snapshot through the observation window at a given time gives a segment of the event stream. As shown in Fig. 3.1, for the current event of Event Type 4, the event sequence in the observation window of size 4 is Event Type 7, Event Type 6, Event Type 3, and Event Type 4. We use 30 predictor variables for the 30 different event types respectively, $(X1, \ldots, X30)$. Each predictor variable represents the existence (1 for existence and 0 for non-existence) of the corresponding event type in the observation window. Hence, for each event in an event stream, we obtain an observation vector of $(X1, \ldots, X30)$. There is one target variable for this data record indicating the intrusiveness of this event. If this event is an intrusive event, the target variable should have the target value of 1 (intrusive); otherwise the target variable should have the target value of 0 (normal).

After this window slides across the entire event stream, a set of data vectors is obtained. In this study, we investigate two different window sizes: 10 and 100 to examine performance differences when different window sizes are used. A decision tree built from a training data set using this feature extraction method is called a Moving Window classifier.

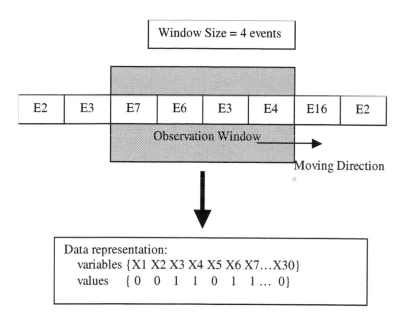

FIG. 3.1. *The Moving Window method of feature extraction.*

In the EWMA Vector method, we also use 30 predictor variables for 30 event types respectively, (X1, ..., X30). In this method, each variable represents the smoothed value of the occurrence frequency of the corresponding event type in the recent past from the current event. That is, (X1, ..., X30) captures the frequency distribution of the 30 event types in the recent past of the event sequence from the current event. The smoothing is based on the Exponentially Weighted Moving Average (EWMA) technique. For the current event n and event type i, we calculate $X_i(n)$ using the following formula:

(3.1)
$$X_i(n) = \lambda * 1 + (1 - \lambda) * X_i(n - 1)$$

if the current event n belongs to the ith event type,

$$X_i(n) = \lambda * 0 + (1 - \lambda) * X_i(n - 1)$$

if the current event n is not the ith event type.

where $X_i(n)$ is the smoothed event frequency of the ith variable for the current event, and λ is a smoothing constant which determines the decay rate.

The larger the λ value, the larger the decay rate. According to formula 3.1, the first event before the current event has the weight of $\lambda*(1-\lambda)$ in the computation of the smoothed event frequency, the second event before the current event has the weight of $\lambda*(1-\lambda)^2$, and so on. Hence, the farther away an event is from the current event, less weight the event receives in computing the frequency distribution of the event types. Hence, in this EWMA Vector method we add the aging factor into the observation value of (X1, ..., X30).

In this study, we initialize $X_i(0)$ to be 0 for i = 1,...,30. We investigate two different values of λ: 0.3 and 0.04 to examine performance differences when different values of λ are used. The λ value of 0.3 is a typical value for the smoothing constant [28], which is approximately equivalent to a window size of about 10 events since the weight for the 9th event from the current event drops to almost zero. The λ value of 0.04 is approximately equivalent to a window size of about 100 events. Hence, for each event in an event stream, we obtain an EWMA vector of (X1,..., X30). There is also one target variable indicating the intrusiveness of this vector. If this event is an intrusive event, the target variable should have the target value of 1 (intrusive); otherwise the target variable should have the target value of 0 (normal). A decision tree built from a training data set using this feature extraction method is called an EWMA vector classifier.

In the State-ID method, we first use a Single Event classifier to classify the single event in an event stream into a state. Each leaf in the Single Event classifier is considered as a state. Using the state information, we transform the original event stream into a state stream. Then we apply the Moving Window classifier to the state stream to produce the state-ID classifier. Two different window sizes of 10 and 100 are investigated.

In summary, for each event in an event stream of a training or testing data set, we use a feature extraction method to obtain a data record with the value(s) of the predictor variable(s). For the training data set, we also assign the value of the target variable for the data record based on whether this event is normal or intrusive. The value of the target variable for the data record of an event in the testing data set is determined using a decision tree classifier. Therefore, using a feature extraction method, we transform an event stream in a training or testing data set into a set of data records that can be processed by the decision tree technique.

3.3. Decision tree classifiers for intrusion signature recognition. In this study, we build and use decision trees for intrusion signature recognition. We call these decision trees decision tree classifiers (DTCs). The application of DTC to intrusion detection needs two phases: training and testing. During training, a decision tree algorithm is used to automatically learn signatures of both intrusive activities and normal activities from the training data of intrusive and normal activities. Both data of intrusive activities and data of normal activities are needed, because without data of normal activities we do not know which patterns of intrusion signature are unique to only intrusive activities. Intrusion signatures are stored in the structure of the decision tree built from the training phase.

Each leaf of the decision tree contains the training examples falling into this leaf. We determine the value of the target variable for each leaf by averaging the target values of the training examples in this leaf. Hence, this value of the target variable falls in $[0, 1]$. The larger the value, the more intrusiveness this leaf represents. Since this value indicates the intrusiveness, we call it the Intrusion Warning (IW) value.

Each leaf in a decision tree can also be considered to represent a state of activities in a computer network system. That is, the decision tree classifies the observed activities in the computer network system into a state of activities. The state information is used in the State-ID method.

During testing, the values of the predictor variables in the data record of an event are passed to a DTC that uses these values of the predictor variables to classify the data record into a leaf of the decision tree. The data record thus takes the IW value of this lead as the value of its target variable.

4. Results and discussions. In this section, we first describe two methods to analyze the detection performance of a DTC. We then present the testing results of various DTCs for the pure data sets. The testing results for the mixed data sets and the noisy data sets are also presented.

4.1. Performance analysis methods. We use two methods to analyze the performance of a DTC. For each event in the testing data, we have the information about the ground truth: whether it is an intrusive or normal event.

One method to analyze the performance of a DTC is to calculate the mean, maximum and minimum of the IW values for all the normal events in the testing data set and the same statistics for all the intrusive events in the testing data set. Two groups of statistics for the normal events and the intrusive events reveal how well the IW values from the DTC separate the intrusive events from the normal events.

Another method is to perform the Receiver Operating Characteristic (ROC) analysis that originates from signal detection theory. Given a signal threshold that is a value in $[0, 1]$, the IW value of each event in the testing data is evaluated to determine whether to signal this event as intrusive. If the IW value is smaller than the signal threshold, no signal is produced; otherwise, we signal this event as intrusive. If a signal is produced on a truly intrusive event, it is a hit. If a signal is produced on a truly normal event, it is a false alarm. For this signal threshold, the hit rate is the number of signals on all the intrusive events divided by the total number of all the intrusive events, and the false alarm rate is the number of signals on all the normal events divided by the total number of all the normal events. Hence, for each possible value in $[0, 1]$ as a signal threshold we can obtain a pair of rates (hit rate, false alarm rate). By plotting these pairs (hit rate, false alarm rate) for various signal thresholds, we obtain a ROC curve. Such a ROC curve can also reveal the detection performance of a DTC as discussed in the following sections.

TABLE 4.1
Statistics for the Single Event classifier using the CHAID algorithm for the pure data sets.

IW Value	Min	Max	Mean	Standard Deviation
Normal	0.00	.462	.200	.113
Intrusive	0.00	1.00	.368	.255

4.2. Performance of the single event classifier for the pure data sets. For the pure data sets, only the CHAID algorithm produces a DTC using the training data. The GINI algorithm fails to produce a DTC using the training data. Table 4.1 presents the descriptive statistics of the IW values of the events in the testing data set. We notice only a small difference in the mean IW value between the normal events and the intrusive events.

Fig. 4.1 shows the ROC curve for the Single Event Classifier. The closer the ROC curve is to the top-left corner of the chart representing the 100% hit rate and the 0% false alarm rate, the better the detection performance of a DTC. The ROC curve in Fig. 4.1 is just a little bit above the diagonal line of the ROC chart that represents the detection performance by random decision making. Although at some signal thresholds the hit rates are high, the false alarm rates at those signal thresholds are also high.

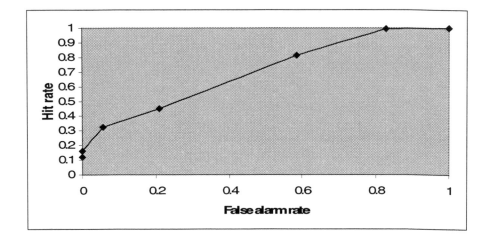

FIG. 4.1. *ROC curve for the Single Event classifier using the CHAID algorithm for the pure data sets.*

4.3. Performance of Moving Window classifiers for the pure data sets. The tree structures produced from the CHAID and GINI algorithms are the same using the Moving Window method of feature extraction and the window size of 10. Table 4.2 shows the statistics for the normal events and intrusive events in the testing data set. It is obvious that the IW values differ considerably

TABLE 4.2

Statistics for the Moving Window classifier using the CHAID and GINI algorithms for the pure data sets.

IW Value	Min	Max	Mean	Standard Deviation
Normal	0.00	.089	.056	.043
Intrusive	.089	1.00	.790	.384

between the normal events and the intrusive events.

Fig. 4.2 shows the ROC curves of the Moving Window classifiers. The detection performance of the Moving Window classifiers is much better than the Single event classifier. For a wide range of signal thresholds, the hit rate remains at about 77% while the false alarm rate is 0%.

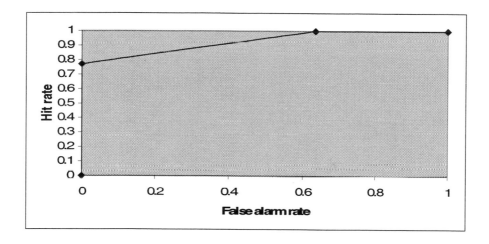

FIG. 4.2. *ROC curves for the Moving Window classifiers using the CHAID and GINI algorithms for the pure data sets.*

4.4. Performance of EWMA Vector Classifiers for the Pure Data Sets. The "EWMA vector" classifiers using the CHAID and GINI algorithms and the λ value of 0.3 produce similar results. Table 4.3 gives the statistics for the classifier based on the CHAID algorithm. The normal events and the intrusive events in the testing data are clearly separated by their IW values. The detection performance of this classifier is even better than that of the Moving Window classifier.

From the ROC curves of the EWMA Vector classifiers as shown in Fig. 4.3, it appears that the EWMA Vector classifiers produce the best detection performance among all the DTC for the pure data sets. For the GINI algorithm, for example, the hit rate remains at about 87% while the false alarm rate is 0% for most signal thresholds.

TABLE 4.3

Statistics for the EWMA vector classifier using the CHAID algorithm for the pure data sets.

IW Value	Min	Max	Mean	Standard Deviation
Normal	0.00	.00	.000	.000
Intrusive	0.00	1.00	.881	.324

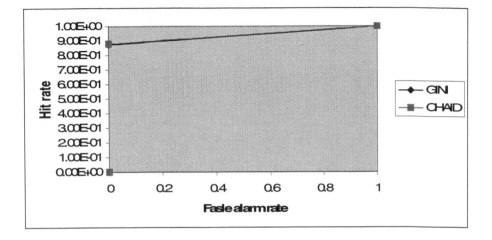

FIG. 4.3. *ROC curves for the EWMA vector classifiers using the CHAID and GINI algorithms for the pure data sets.*

4.5. Performance of State-ID classifiers for the pure data sets . For the window size of 10, the statistics in Table 4.4 show that the difference in the IW values between the normal events and the intrusive events is very large, comparable to that from the Moving Window classifier. The standard deviations are small here. This implies that we can detect the normal events and the intrusive events accurately.

Fig. 4.4 shows the ROC curves for the State-ID classifiers using the CHAID and GINI algorithms respectively. For a range of signal thresholds, the hit rates of these classifiers all reach around 96% while the false alarm rates stay at about 6.6%. Therefore, the state information from the Single Event classifier improves the detection performance of the Moving Window classifier.

4.6. Performance of DTCs for a different window size and a different smoothing constant for the pure data sets. The above testing results are for the λ value of 0.3 or the window size of 10. Fig. 4.5 shows the ROC curve of the EWMA Vector classifier for the λ value of 0.04 using the CHAID algorithm in comparison with that of the EWMA Vector classifier for the λ value of 0.3 for the pure data sets. There is a slight performance difference between these two ROC curves in Fig. 4.5. From the ROC curves of the Moving Window

TABLE 4.4
Statistics for the state-ID classifiers for the pure data sets.

Classifiers	Mean/ Normal	Mean/ Attack	S.D./ Normal	S.D./ Attack
Normal	.066	.861	.219	.224
Intrusive	.059	.841	.210	.294

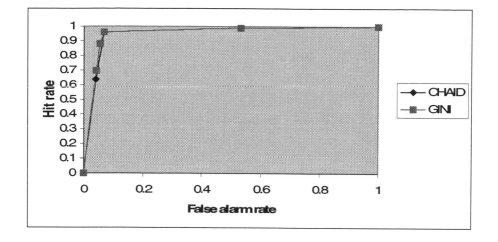

FIG. 4.4. *ROC curves for the State-ID classifiers using the CHAID and GINI algorithms for the pure data sets.*

classifiers for different moving window sizes in Fig. 4.6, it appears that the longer window size produces better detection performance for the pure data sets.

4.7. Performance of the EWMA vector classifiers for different data sets. Since the EWMA Vector method produces the best performance among all the DTCs for the pure data sets, the EWMA Vector method is tested for two other data sets to examine performance impact of noises in data: the mixed data sets and the noisy data sets. The ROC curves of these classifiers are shown in Fig. 4.7 and Fig. 4.8 in comparison with the ROC curve for the pure data sets. It appears that the detection performance of the EWMA classifiers for the mixed data sets and the noisy data sets degrades sharply in comparison with that of the EWMA classifier for the pure data sets. In the EWMA Vector method, the observation value of each predictor variable for the current event depends on not only the current event but also the events before the current events in the recent past. Hence, noises in data likely reduce the difference in the observation value between the normal events and the intrusive events, thus degrading the detection performance.

From the ROC curves in Fig. 4.7 and Fig. 4.8, it appears that the detection performance of the EWMA Vector classifier for the noisy data sets seems a little better than that for the mixed data sets. This implies that when the noise

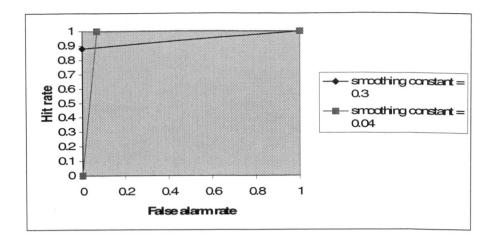

FIG. 4.5. *ROC curves for the EWMA Vector classifiers with different smoothing constants using the CHAID algorithm.*

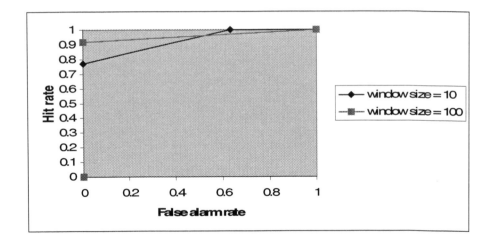

FIG. 4.6. *ROC curves of the Moving Window classifiers for different window sizes using the CHAID algorithm for the pure data sets.*

level of the testing data is similar to the noise level of the training data, better detection performance may be produced.

5. Summary. In this study, different decision tree classifiers based on different feature extraction methods have been designed and tested. We compare the detection performance of these decision tree classifiers. From the analysis and comparison of their detection performance, decision tree classifiers seem to show a potential for intrusion signature recognition.

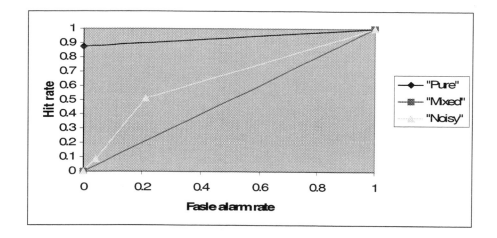

FIG. 4.7. *ROC curves of the EWMA Vector classifiers using the GINI algorithm for three kinds of data sets.*

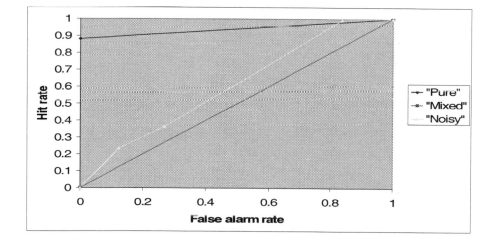

FIG. 4.8. *ROC curves of the EWMA Vector classifiers using the CHAID algorithm for different kinds of data sets.*

This study provides some insights into the application of the decision tree technique and possibly other data mining techniques to intrusion detection. First of all, different methods of selecting features of raw activity data appear to have a large impact on the detection performance. Secondly, parameters such as the window size and factors such as noises in data can also affect the detection performance of DTCs.

There are still issues that need to be investigated, including the scalability of decision tree algorithms for large data sets and the ability of decision tree algorithms to perform the incremental learning, because new data of normal and intrusive activities may become available over time. Since the amount of audit data from a computer network system can be huge, DTCs must be computationally feasible for large data sets. There exist decision tree algorithms that support incremental learning. However, they are not scalable to large data sets.

Acknowledgement. This work is sponsored in part by the Defense Advanced Research Project Agency (DARPA)/Air Force Research Laboratory (AFRL-Rome)under grant number F30602-99-1-0506. The U.S. government is authorized to reproduce and distribute reprints for governmental purposes notwithstanding any copyright annotation thereon. The views and conclusions contained herein are those of the authors and should not be interpreted as necessarily representing the official policies or endorsements, either express or implied, of DARPA, AFRL-Rome, or the U.S. Government.

REFERENCES

[1] R. HEADY, G. LUGER, A. MACCABE, AND M. SERVILLA, *The Architecture of a Network Level Intrusion Detection System*, Technical Report CS90-20, Department of Computer Science, University of New Mexico, 1990.

[2] R. GRAHAM, *FAQ: Network Intrusion Detection Systems*, http://www.robertgraham.com/ pubs/network-intrusion-detection.html, 2001.

[3] T. ESCAMILLA, *Intrusion Detection: Network Security beyond the Firewall*, John Wiley & Sons, New York, 1998.

[4] E. A. FISCH AND G. B. WHITE, *Secure Computers and Networks*, CRC Press LLC, Boca Ration, Florida, 2000.

[5] E. S. RAYMOND, *How To Become A Hacker*, http://www.tuxedo.org/~esr/faqs/hacker-howto.html, 2001.

[6] D. DENNING, *An Intrusion-detection Model*, IEEE Transactions on Software Engineering, 13(1987), pp. 222-232.

[7] D. A. FRINCKE AND M. HUANG, *Recent Advances in Intrusion Detection Systems*, Computer Networks, 34(2001), pp. 541-545.

[8] P. PORRAS, *STAT - A State Transition Analysis Tool for Intrusion Detection*, Technical Report TRCS93-25, Computer Science Department, University of California at Santa Barbara, 1993.

[9] S. KUMAR AND E. H. SPAFFORD, *An Application of Pattern Matching in Intrusion Detection*, Technical Report CSD-TR-94-013, The COAST Project, Dept. of Computer Sciences, Purdue University, West Lafayette, IN, USA, 1994.

[10] S. E. SMAHA, *Haystack: An intrusion detection system*, Proceedings of the IEEE 4th Aerospace Computer Security Applications Conference, pp. 37-44, 1988.

[11] P. G. NEUMANN AND P. A. PORRAS, *Experience with EMERALD to date*, Proceedings of First USENIX Workshop on Intrusion Detection and Network Monitoring, pp. 73-80, Santa Clara, CA, 1999.

[12] D. ENDLER, *Intrusion detection: Applying machine learning to Solaris audit data*, Proceedings of 14th Annual Computer Security Applications Conference, pp. 268-279, 1998.

[13] W. LEE, S. J. STOLFO, AND K. MOK, *A data mining framework for building intrusion detection models*, Proceedings of 1999 IEEE Symposium on Security and Privacy, pp. 120-132, 1999.

[14] T. F. LUNT, *IDES: An intelligent system for detecting intruders*, Proceedings of the Symposium: Computer Security, Treat and Countermeasures, 1990.

[15] S. FORREST, S. A. HOFMEYR, AND A. SOMAYATI, *Computer Immunology*, Communications of the ACM, 40(1997), pp. 88 96.
[16] R. LIPPMANN, D. FRIED, I. GRAF, J. HAINES, K. KENDALL, D. MCCLUNG, D. WEBER, S. WEBSTER, D. WYSCHOGROD, R. CUNNINGHAM, AND M. ZISSMAN, *Evaluating intrusion detection systems: The 1998 DARPA off-line intrusion detection evaluation*, Proceedings of the DARPA Information Survivability Conference and Exposion, IEEE Computer Society, Los Alamitos, pp. 12-26, 2000.
[17] R. LIPPMANN, J. W. HAINES, D. FRIED, I. GRAF, J. KORBA, K. DAS, *The 1999 DARPA off-line intrusion detection evaluation*, Computer Networks, 34(2000), pp. 579-595.
[18] R. G. BACE, *Intrusion Detection*, Macmillan Technical Publishing, Indianapolis, 2000.
[19] S. AXELSSON, *Intrusion Detection Systems: A Survey and Taxonomy*, Technical Report, Department of Computer Engineering, Chalmers University of Technology, Goteborg, Sweden, 2000.
[20] H. DEBAR, M. DACIER, AND A. WESPI, *Towards a taxonomy of intrusion-detection systems*, Computer Networks, 31(1999), pp. 805-822.
[21] C. SINCLAIR, L. PIERCE, AND S. MATZNER, *An application of machine learning to network intrusion detection*, Proceedings of 15th Annual Computer Security Applications Conference (ACSAC '99), pp. 371-377, 1999.
[22] T. MITCHELL, *Machine Learning*, WCB/McGraw-Hill, 1997.
[23] L. BREIMAN, J. FRIEDMAN, R. OLSHEN, AND C. STONE, *Classification and Regression Trees*, Wadsworth Inc., 1984.
[24] S. R. SAFAVIAN AND D. LANDGREBE, *A survey of decision tree classifier methodology*, IEEE Transactions on Systems, Man and Cybernetics, 21(1991), pp. 660-674.
[25] S. L. CRAWFORD, *Extensions to the CART algorithm*, Int. J. Man-Machine Studies, 31(1989), pp. 197-217.
[26] SPSS INC., *User's Guide of AnswerTree 2.0*, Chicago, Illinois, 1998.
[27] P. J. BROCKWELL AND R. A. DAVIS, *Time Series: Theory and Methods*, Springer-Verlag, 1987.
[28] T. P. RYAN, *Statistical Methods for Quality Improvement*, New York: John Wiley & Sons.

EFFICIENT SUPPORT FOR PIPELINING IN SOFTWARE DISTRIBUTED SHARED MEMORY SYSTEMS*

KARTHIK BALASUBRAMANIAN
DAVID K. LOWENTHAL
DEPARTMENT OF COMPUTER SCIENCE
UNIVERSITY OF GEORGIA
{KAR,DKL}@CS.UGA.EDU

Abstract. Though more difficult to program, distributed-memory parallel machines provide greater scalability than their shared-memory counterparts. Software Distributed Shared Memory (SDSM) systems provide the abstraction of shared memory on a distributed machine. While SDSMs provide an attractive programming model, they currently can not efficiently support all classes of scientific applications. One such class are those with recurrences that cause dependencies across processors or nodes. A popular solution to such problems is to use *pipelining*, which breaks the computation into blocks; each processor performs the computation of a block, which enables the next processor in the pipeline to compute its corresponding block. Once the pipeline is filled, the computation of blocks proceeds in parallel. While pipelining is useful, it is not efficiently supported by current SDSM systems.

This paper presents an approach to integrating pipelining into SDSM systems. We describe our design and implementation of one-way pipelining in a SDSM. The key idea is to retain the shared-memory model, but design the extensions such that the execution will mimic what would be done in an explicit message-passing program. We show that one-way pipelining is superior to the two most common ways to program pipelined applications, which are distributed locks and explicit matrix transposition. Finally, we show that one-way pipelining is competitive with a hand-coded, explicit message-passing program.

1. Introduction. The computational requirements of many scientific applications have created a need for high-performance parallel architectures. These architectures can be broadly categorized as *shared-memory multiprocessors* and *distributed-memory multicomputers*. Distributed-memory machines provide greater scalability and higher performance than their shared-memory counterparts. However, writing a parallel program for a distributed-memory machine is more complicated because it requires the use of explicit message passing to communicate between the processors. To the parallel programmer (or compiler), the shared-memory model is simpler than the distributed-memory model.

Software distributed shared memory (SDSM) systems strive to provide the best features of each of the two kinds of parallel architectures—the power and scalability of the distributed model with the programming ease of the shared model. A SDSM system provides the abstraction of the shared-memory model on a distributed-memory machine—that is, it eliminates explicit interprocessor communication. The model provided by the SDSM system is similar to that of traditional virtual memory. The SDSM provides a virtual address space, divided into pages, that is global to all processors (nodes). A reference by a node to non-resident data generates a *page fault* that is trapped by the SDSM. The SDSM pages the data into the node's memory by sending a message to the node that

---

*THIS WORK WAS SUPPORTED BY NATIONAL SCIENCE FOUNDATION CAREER GRANT CCR-9733063.

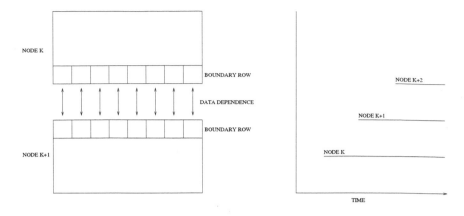

FIG. 1.1. *Computation with a cross-node dependence. Note that after the last node starts computation, all nodes run in parallel.*

has the page. Hence, internode communication is done *implicitly* by the SDSM system in a manner similar to how disk I/O is managed in paged operating systems.

Recently, SDSM systems have received attention as attractive compiler targets[KT97, CDLZ97]. This is because it is much easier to generate code without having to determine at compile time whether data is local or not. Furthermore, when communication patterns cannot be determined at compile time, compilers often have to generate code with all to all communication, which is prohibitively expensive. On the other hand, with a SDSM backend, communication is performed only on demand.

Unfortunately, current SDSM systems are not universal enough to serve as general-purpose compiler backends. In particular, many scientific programs exhibit recurrences in their problem formulations. These recurrences give rise to *cross-node dependencies*, which result when, between synchronization points, an update to a data element on one (node) depends on the value of a data element on another (node). The dependence enforces an ordering on the execution of the loop as well as a message transfer between nodes. These dependencies tend to slow down parallel execution and sometimes even serialize the loop. This paper focuses on cross-node dependencies. These types of dependencies are quite common in scientific codes, including ADI integration, 2-d FFTs, and implicit hydrodynamics codes. A computation that has this kind of dependence is shown pictorially in Figure 1.1.

In a SDSM system, one solution to cross-node dependencies is to compute the transpose of the matrix before the loop so that cross-node dependencies are eliminated. After the loop is executed, the matrix is transformed to its original state by computing another transpose. This solution, although simple to implement on a SDSM system, is typically not viable due to excessive communication overhead. An alternative solution is to *pipeline* the loop. Software pipelines

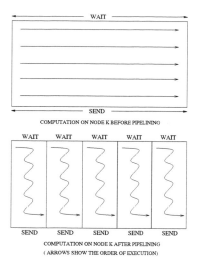

FIG. 1.2. *Pipelined computation. The computation proceeds by blocks instead of by rows.*

provide an efficient solution in computations that exhibit recurrences that cause cross-node dependencies. Instead of proceeding by rows, the computation proceeds by blocks. This reduces the time that a node has to wait before it can begin the computation. Figure 1.2 pictorially shows a pipelined computation.

However, implementing explicit pipeline parallelism in a SDSM system is not straightforward. In particular, it requires (1) allowing nodes to communicate without sending explicit messages, (2) sending the minimum amount of data, and (3) avoiding thrashing, a well-known SDSM problem.

This paper presents an approach to pipelined parallelism for a SDSM system. We have extended Filaments [FLA94, LFA96], a software kernel that provides a SDSM, to support pipelined parallelism. We provide the user (or compiler) with all functions needed to pipeline a program. Our implementation runs on a cluster of workstations connected by a dedicated Fast Ethernet. Performance results show that our one-way pipeline implementation achieves good speedup and is competitive (e.g., just over 10% slower on 8 nodes) with an explicit message-passing program, which is more difficult to write. Furthermore, our one-way pipeline is superior to using either locks or an explicit transpose, which are the two primary ways most programmers implement shared-memory pipelined programs. Finally, applications that do not require pipelining are not affected by our support for pipelining.

The remainder of this paper is organized as follows. Section 2 gives an overview of the concepts and terminology relevant to the work presented in this paper. It also presents related work. Section 3 briefly describes the Filaments package. Section 4 discusses the implementation of one-way pipelines and compares it with distributed locks. Section 5 presents performance of both implementations and Section 6 concludes.

2. Overview and Related Work. In this section, we give an overview of concepts and terminology related to our work. We describe both SDSMs and pipelining and then the difficulty involved in integrating the two. Finally, we present related work.

2.1. Software Distributed Shared Memory Systems. As discussed above, distributed-memory machines deliver high performance and scalability, but have a complicated programming model. A *software distributed shared memory* (SDSM) system provides an abstraction of shared memory on a distributed machine. On page-based SDSM systems, communication between nodes occurs implicitly using page faults. The basic principle behind a SDSM system is an extension of virtual memory. The SDSM provides a virtual address space that the nodes in the distributed system share. Application programs use this memory as conventional virtual memory. The SDSM takes care of paging the data between the memories of the different nodes on demand.

Any node can access any location in the shared address space. A SDSM system implements the mapping between the local memory and the shared address space, which is partitioned into pages; a memory reference by a node generates a page fault when the page is not resident. Such a *page fault* is trapped by the SDSM system, which acquires a copy of the requested page by sending a message to the node that has the page.

A key issue involved in building a SDSM system is solving the *memory coherence problem*; there are a number of strategies that can be used. These strategies are usually referred to as *page consistency protocols*; here, we discuss the write-invalidate protocol [LH89], where each page has either a single writer or multiple readers.

With write-invalidate, when a node incurs a page fault, the SDSM moves a copy of the page to the node that faulted. If the fault is on a write, all other copies are invalidated, and the faulting node is given write permission. If the fault is on a read, the access permission becomes read-only on all copies (which may involve changing permissions).

Another key issue is avoiding thrashing, which occurs when a single page "ping-pongs" between two nodes. It is caused by false sharing, which occurs when at least two nodes have a copy of a page, and at least one is writing. Write-shared protocols [CBZ91] have been developed to tolerate thrashing in the case that there are no *true dependencies*, which occurs between two statements S_1 and S_2 when (1) S_1 precedes S_2 and (2) S_1 writes to a memory location that S_2 reads. Our applications all exhibit true dependencies, so we cannot use write-shared protocols.

2.2. Pipelined Parallelism. Typically, in scientific applications, parallelism is extracted from loops because that is where most of the time is spent. Iterations of such loops are executed in parallel to achieve speedup over the sequential program. However, a number of these scientific applications exhibit recurrences that give rise to *data dependencies*. These dependencies enforce an ordering on the execution of the iterations in the loop where they occur, some-

```
for iter := 1 to NUMITERS {
  /* row sweep */
  for i := 0 to N-1
   for j := 0 to N-1
     X[i][j] := F(X[i][j], X[i][j-1], A[i], B[i])
  /* column sweep */
  for i := 0 to N-1
   for j := 0 to N-1
     X[i][j] := F(X[i][j], X[i-1][j], A[i], B[i])
}
```

FIG. 2.1. *Outline of sequential ADI program*

```
for iter := 1 to NUMITERS {
  /* row sweep */
  for i := start to end
   for j := 0 to N-1
     X[i][j] := F(X[i][j], X[i][j-1], A[i], B[i])

  /* column sweep */
  for jj := 0 to N-1 by blocksize
    if (myId != 0)
      LockAcquire(block[myProcessor][jj/blocksize]);
    for i := start to end
      for j := jj to jj+blocksize-1
        X[i][j] := F(X[i][j], X[i-1][j], A[i], B[i])
    if (myId != p-1)
      LockRelease(block[myProcessor+1][jj/blocksize]);
}
```

FIG. 2.2. *Pipelined shared-memory ADI program. Variables* **start** *and* **end** *are local to each processor and based on the number of participating processors such that the work is divided evenly. A shared two-dimensional array of locks is used for synchronization; an acquire is done before a block and a release is done afterwards.*

times even forcing sequentialization of the execution of the entire loop.

Figure 2.1 shows a section of the Alternate Direction Implicit (ADI) integration program. Assume that the data (matrices) are distributed in groups of consecutive rows during the row sweep, which is what a typical parallelizing compiler would choose. This allows the row sweep to be executed in parallel without incurring any communication. However, in the column sweep, there is a dependence since the value of $X[i][j]$ depends on the value of $X[i-1][j]$. This means that node k must acquire a value from node $k-1$ in order to compute each value of its first row.

```
if (myId == 0)
  send appropriate parts of arrays X, A, and B to each node
else
  receive appropriate parts of arrays X, A, and B from node 0

for iter := 1 to NUMITERS {
  /* row sweep */
  for i := start to end
    for j := 0 to N-1
      X[i][j] := F(X[i][j], X[i][j-1], A[i], B[i])

  /* column sweep */
  for jj := 0 to N-1 by blocksize
    if (myId != 0)
      receive X[start-1][jj:jj+blocksize] from previous node
    for i := start to end
      for j := jj to jj+blocksize-1
        X[i][j] := F(X[i][j], X[i-1][j], A[i], B[i])
    if (myId != p-1)
      send X[end][jj:jj+blocksize] to next node
}

if (myId == 0)
  accumulate arrays X, A, and B from each node
else
  send my part arrays X, A, and B to node 0
```

FIG. 2.3. *Pipelined, explicit message-passing version of ADI program. Variables* **start** *and* **end** *are local to each node and based on the number of participating nodes such that the work is divided evenly. Note that writing an explicit message passing program forces the programmer or compiler to distribute data before the computation as well as accumulate it afterwards. Several other things (not shown here) must be done, such as proper memory allocation per node and translation of global to local indices.*

There are three primary solutions to this problem:

- serialize the second loop
- compute the transpose of the matrix before and after the column sweep phase and perform the second loop in parallel without any communication, or
- pipeline the computation, which avoids changing the data distribution.

Serializing the second loop is a simple solution but fails to extract parallelism. The second solution, computing the transpose, is highly inefficient; we show evidence of this in Section 5. The third solution, pipelining the computation, is the one that this paper discusses in detail. Software pipelining is a popular method to extract parallelism from problems that exhibit recurrences, such as the one shown in Figure 2.1.

Pipelined shared-memory and distributed-memory programs for ADI are shown in Figures 2.2 and 2.3. The computation is split up into blocks; each processor/node performs the computation blockwise. In the shared-memory program, synchronization is performed by acquiring and releasing appropriate locks; on the other hand, in the distributed-memory program, message receives and sends are done. This allows a a processor/node to start before the preceding processor/node has completed the computation on all its rows. Once the pipeline is filled, the computation of blocks on different processors/nodes proceeds in parallel.

2.3. The Problem. Although a pipeline can be naturally described in terms of explicit sends and receives, it is still simpler to program with shared memory. This is because no data need be sent; message passing is notoriously difficult to use correctly, especially in initialization and finalization code (as shown in Figure 2.3). (Furthermore, as discussed below, compilers can generate code much more easily for a shared-memory backend.) The shared-memory SUIF compiler [HAA+96], for example, compiles codes with dependencies into pipelined codes similar to the one shown in Figure 2.2.

As a SDSM system provides the abstraction of shared-memory on a distributed machine, one might expect it to be able to support programming pipelined applications with locks or semaphores. In other words, the program in Figure 2.2 might be expected to work correctly and efficiently on a SDSM. Unfortunately, this is not the case. Programming pipelines in current SDSMs as one would in a shared-memory multiprocessor can easily lead to (1) more than the minimum amount of data being sent, (2) thrashing, and (3) non-optimal (2-way) communication. To understand why, note that in a SDSM system, the acquisition of a single block (likely much smaller than a page) will result in acquisition of an entire page. Furthermore, when a block is smaller than a page, we have a situation where two nodes are accessing different blocks, but both blocks are on the same page. Because one node is writing, thrashing could result. Finally, the SDSM model is one of request/reply; a page fault causes a request, and the page is sent in reply. This is in contrast to the more efficient distributed-memory model, in which nodes simply block until they receive the boundary data from the previous node and then send the boundary data to the next node when they are done.

Our goal is to retain the SDSM environment—no explicit message passing—while still sending the minimum amount of data and no extra consistency messages. This paper discusses the design, implementation, and performance of a SDSM system that *efficiently* supports pipelined parallelism.

2.4. Related Work.

SDSM Systems. There is an abundance of related work on hardware and software distributed shared memory systems. An excellent survey appears in Iftode's dissertation [Ift98], in which SDSM research is divided into four areas:

consistency models, protocols, applications, and architectural support. This paper focuses on software DSM (SDSM), so we will outline the most relevant related work from the first three areas; additionally, we make some remarks about performance. Further, within the section on applications, we will focus on compiler integration with SDSM systems.

Consistency. The first SDSM system, described in the classic paper by Li and Hudak [LH89], used sequential consistency. This means that every write to memory must be immediately made visible to all processes. While this extends the memory model programmers expect on a single processor, it results in excessive and unnecessary consistency operations in an SDSM environment. Consider the situation where two processors access different data on the same memory page, and one of them writes. The need to make the write immediately visible causes an invalidation of the reader's copy of the page. The reader will immediately incur a page fault and obtain a copy of a page, and then the cycle will repeat. This behavior is known as thrashing.

To reduce consistency communication in SDSM systems, it is necessary to relax the memory consistency model. Munin [CBZ91] used *release consistency* to delay consistency until a release point (either a barrier arrival or a lock release). Treadmarks [KDCZ94] further delayed communication using lazy release consistency. Another protocol that further relaxes the consistency model is entry consistency [BZS93], where the programmer binds shared data to a lock, and a release of the lock automatically propagates that data to the acquiring node. Finally, scope consistency is similar to entry consistency, except that the binding between a lock and the associated is achieved dynamically, through scoping induced by synchronization variables [IPL96]. An alternative consistency model can be derived from using an integrated SDSM/message passing system [KF94]; such a system allows no consistency where appropriate (but requires messages in that case, which is contrary to one of our goals). A comprehensive survey of different memory consistency models can be found in [Mos93].

Protocols. With a relaxed memory consistency model, page consistency protocols can be developed that improve efficiency. For example, given the ability to delay visibility of writes until consistency points, Munin developed a multiple writer protocol that *cloned* write-shared pages; at synchronization points, diffs between the original and modified pages are computed and exchanged, bringing all nodes' copies up to date. Treadmarks delayed making a page consistent even further, waiting until a node actually referenced that page after a synchronization point. Home-based protocols designate a home node for each page; all updates are propagated to that node eagerly [IDFL96]. This allows communication that linear in the number of nodes, but can result in more total communication.

A slightly different (and often better) approach to allowing multiple writers is to eliminate false sharing. This was done with the writer-owns protocol [FA96]. The basic idea is to move data that is causing thrashing to a new SDSM page, which uses extra memory but does not require any diffs to be sent. This allows sequential consistency on pages on which thrashing is not occurring. Another approach that allows sequential consistency while avoiding large amounts of thrashing is to use multiple virtual copies of SDSM variables, where each is mapped to a different page. This is the approach taken by Millipede [IS99], which effectively allows small pages. Similar ideas have been developed by Zwaenopoel et al [HYW+00].

Integrating Compilers with SDSM. Several researchers have recently studied integrating compilers with SDSM systems. Cox et al. [CDLZ97] use regular sections to determine when explicit messages can be used instead of page faults. They follow on with extensions to support irregular applications [LCD+97]. Keleher and Tseng eliminate consistency information, and reduce the number of barriers needed [KT97]. Ioannadis and Dwarkadas use compiler information along with a runtime system to adaptively distribute pages to nodes [ID98]. Their system handles single-phase applications. Howard and Lowenthal [HL00] use an integrated compiler/runtime system to distribute pages to nodes in multiple phase applications.

Performance. Several researchers have looked into the important issue of performance comparison of SDSM and message passing. Freeh et al. [FLA94] gave performance of four SDSM applications compared to message passing, and showed that when using multithreading and dynamic load balancing, the SDSM programs were competitive. Lu et al. [LDCZ95] executed nine applications, finding that the difference ranged from insignificant, when the degree of sharing is small, to significant, when it is large. The Strings system, a SDSM for clusters of multiprocessors, was shown to provide performance close to that of message passing [RCJM99].

Pipelining. Pipelining computations can provide an efficient solution to cross-node dependencies in loops. As a result, a number of parallelizing compilers and systems use pipelining to exploit parallelism. There is a wealth of related work on pipelining [AK87, BCG+95, HLKL97, KTG95, Lov77, VSM96]; this section presents some of it.

Before support for pipelining was built into parallelizing compilers, a number of researchers wrote programs that were pipelined by "hand". The computations in these application programs were pipelined by explicitly passing messages.

An optimizing Fortran D compiler developed at Rice University [Tse93] uses a number of optimization techniques to generate efficient parallel programs. This compiler analyzes programs, performs optimizations and generates code. The compiler uses optimization techniques that are guided by data dependencies. One of the optimization techniques used by the compiler to exploit parallelism is pipelining. The compiler applies mechanisms such as loop fusion, loop interchange and strip mining to pipeline the computation of the loop. Two of the techniques that the compiler uses to exploit pipeline parallelism are fine- and coarse-grain pipelining. With fine-grain pipelining, loop interchange is used to minimize the granularity of the pipeline, maximizing pipeline parallelism at the cost of increasing the communication overhead. Coarse-grain pipelining attempts to balance the parallelism with communication overhead by using loop transformations to increase the granularity of the pipeline.

PARADIGM [BCG+95] is a parallelizing compiler built for distributed-memory multicomputers. PARADIGM performs a number of optimizations to generate efficient parallel code. It uses coarse-grain pipelining to exploit parallelism in loops with cross-node dependencies. The system uses an execution time estimate to compute the total cost of execution of the loop. This total cost is then minimized with respect to the block size to select the granularity for the pipeline. Once this granularity has been calculated, various loop transformations are used to change the granularity of the pipeline to improve execution time.

Other recent compiler work has focused on using *multipartitioning*, which is a more efficient alternative to pipelining, for problems with directional sweeps only [CM00]. However, this scheme does not generalize to problems with dependencies in multiple dimensions.

The block size can be crucial to the performance of a pipelined parallel program. A smaller block size results in smaller idle time per node, but increases the communication overhead. A larger block size has the reverse effect—it reduces the communication overhead, but results in a larger pipeline fill time. The ideal block size is one that will minimize the completion time. A run-time system [LJ99] has been developed to analyze and choose an effective block size for pipelining using explicit messages. The system analyzes the program on the first iteration and based on timing results, it chooses an effective block size (which can be nonuniform) for the computation. The best block size found is then used for the remainder of the computation.

3. Filaments. Filaments is a software kernel that efficiently supports a fine-grain, shared-memory programming model on a range of architectures. It includes very lightweight threads, called filaments, as well as a multithreaded software distributed shared memory (SDSM) and an efficient communication protocol. This section describes only those parts of Filaments relevant to this paper, which are the SDSM and reliable UDP communication protocol.

3.1. Filaments Distributed Shared Memory System. The SDSM in Filaments is implemented entirely in software. Hence, it is inexpensive and extremely flexible. With a relatively small amount of operating system support, it can be ported to different hardwares and operating systems. The Filaments SDSM is already supported on SPARC/Solaris, PentiumPro/Solaris, and PentiumPro/Linux.

The SDSM divides the address space of the node into two sections—a shared section and a private section. The shared section, currently divided into 4K pages, contains the user data that is shared by all the nodes. The private section contains the data that is local to a node; for example, program code, local variables in the program, etc.

There are two events that could occur in the SDSM system: remote page fault and message pending. A message pending event is generated when a node receives a message. It is handled asynchronously by an event handler routine that is called when a SIGIO signal is generated (by the incoming message). A remote page fault occurs when a thread on a node accesses a remote page.

The pages in the SDSM are protected using the mprotect call. When a thread tries to access a remote page, a SIGSEGV signal is generated. A signal handler traps this signal and sends out a request for the remote page and also suspends the thread. It then calls the scheduler, which will execute another thread. When the remote page request is satisfied, the scheduler places the faulting thread in the ready queue so that it can be executed again. Since there are a number of threads that can be executed, the SDSM system can support several outstanding page requests. Indeed, the ability to overlap communication with computation is the main difference between Filaments and other SDSMs.

Filaments can support several *page consistency protocols*; currently, it supports *migratory, write-invalidate and implicit-invalidate*. The migratory protocol keeps exactly one copy of each page. The page moves from node to node when necessary. With write-invalidate, multiple read-only copies of a page are allowed, but the copies are invalidated explicitly when one of them is written. Implicit-invalidate is a more efficient version of the write-invalidate protocol. With implicit-invalidate, all read-only copies of a page are implicitly invalidated at each synchronization point. Hence, explicit invalidate messages are unnecessary. However, implicit-invalidate works only with regular problems with stable data sharing patterns. In this paper we focus on (and modify) the write-invalidate protocol.

3.2. Communication Model. A SDSM requires reliable communication as well as low overhead. Filaments uses the User Datagram Protocol (UDP) which is an unreliable but fast protocol. On UNIX, the choice is between TCP and UDP. Although TCP is reliable, it does not scale well with the number of nodes. UDP is unreliable but does scale well. Additionally, it is slightly faster than TCP and also supports broadcast messages. Filaments, therefore, uses UDP with reliability built on top of it. The result is a fast and reliable protocol.

There are two kinds of messages: request and reply. A node sends out a request to which another node replies. If the request is lost or delayed, the sending node retransmits the request. This means that the each request message sent has to be buffered. However, the request messages are small, so buffering is not expensive. The request message is added to a list of sent messages and each time a reply is received, the corresponding request message is removed from the list. Our version of UDP does not buffer SDSM page data. Instead, only the actual reply is buffered and the data part of the reply is constructed from the contents of the page at the time of retransmission. This is possible because all nodes wait at synchronization points until all outstanding requests are satisfied, which in turn means that if the program has no race conditions, a request is always satisfied by a reply with a consistent copy of the page [FLA94].

4. Implementation. This section presents the implementation of pipelining in a software distributed shared memory (SDSM). We implemented one-way pipelines that are written using a shared-memory model, while the execution model is that of distributed-memory. For comparison, we also implemented distributed locks (which is the traditional "shared-memory" way to pipeline). First, we discuss elements common to both implementations. Then, we discuss the user interface and implementation of one-way pipelining. Note that we initially assume only one array and an upward dependence; later, we relax these restrictions. Next, we discuss the user interface and implementation of distributed locks. As this is borrowed from Midway [ZSB94] and used only for comparison to one way pipelining, its description is brief. Finally, we briefly discuss integration of a compiler with our one-way SDSM pipelines.

4.1. Common Elements. The simplest solution to SDSM pipelining would be to force a node to wait, with some blocking primitive, until the previous node has finished with the computation. Then we could let the SDSM acquire the data implicitly by faulting on the corresponding block of data from the preceding node's last row. However, there are three problems with this approach. First, as each last (bottommost) row on a node is referred to by *two* nodes, the page(s) on which the last row is located will be transferred between the two nodes a large number of times. For example, suppose the last row takes one page and is divided into $n > 1$ blocks; consider the first two nodes (which share a row). After computation of the first block on the first node, the second node would fault on the entire page. Hence, we don't have the minimum amount of data being transferred, because we need a page fault on the (same) page for *each* of the n blocks. Second, we have two nodes accessing the page, and one writing. This situation is well-known to cause thrashing. Note that using a write-shared protocol is not possible here, because there is a true dependence. (Write-shared works only when the concurrent accesses are to completely disjoint memory locations.) Finally, two-way communication is necessary when using traditional SDSM protocols.

The solution to the first two problems, for both one-way pipelines and locks, requires a new page consistency protocol (PCP) for Filaments that we call *pipeline-invalidate*. Pipeline-invalidate is the same as write-invalidate except that it marks the last row of each node as READ/WRITE. This ensures that a node will not generate a page fault when it refers to the data on the last row of the preceding node. Note that with pipeline-invalidate, the data now has to be explicitly sent to the node requiring it as there will be no page fault on boundary rows. Further, synchronization must be inserted to ensure that computation on a node begins only after the appropriate data has been received. There are two different ways to provide this synchronization: *one-way pipelines* and *distributed locks*. The remainder of this section describes the implementation of these two approaches in detail. Each approach has two subsections: one describing the user interface and the other describing the implementation.

```
/* SDSM initialization code omitted */

/* parameters to SDSMInitPipeline:
   pipeline id, number of elements, block size, array name
*/

SDSMInitPipeline(1, n, blocksize, X)

for iter := 1 to NUMITERS {
  /* row sweep */
  for i := start to end
    for j := 0 to N-1
      X[i][j] := F(X[i][j], X[i][j-1], A[i], B[i])

  /* column sweep */
  for jj := 0 to N-1 by blocksize
    if (myId != 0)
      BlockWait(1);  /* parameter id pipeline id */
    for i := start to end
      for j := jj to jj+blocksize-1
        X[i][j] := F(X[i][j], X[i-1][j], A[i], B[i])
    if (myId != p-1)
      BlockDone(1);  /* parameter is pipeline id */
}
```

FIG. 4.1. *Pipelined ADI program using our SDSM system. Variables* **start** *and* **end** *are local to each processor and based on the number of participating processors such that the work is divided evenly. The system tracks what data needs to be sent or received at a BlockWait() or BlockDone() call and handles it implicitly. Furthermore, BlockWait() delays the caller until the necessary data has been received. It is important to note that the only modifications to our SDSM programming model are the three function calls.*

4.2. One-Way Pipelines.

4.2.1. User Interface.
Our modified Filaments SDSM provides the user with a simple API for implementing a pipelined program. The API consists of InitPipeline, BlockWait, and BlockDone. The user creates a pipeline for an array using the InitPipeline function call. The parameters passed to this function are:
- id of pipeline
- number of blocks
- size and start address of array

The function BlockWait forces a node to wait for a block of data from the preceding node and returns when the SDSM receives the data from the preceding node. All nodes except the first call BlockWait. The function BlockDone marks

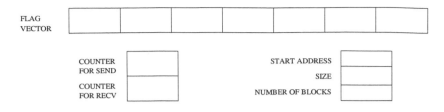

FIG. 4.2. *One pipeline on a node. In this example there are seven blocks. There is a flag vector to keep track of potentially multiple messages, and separate counters indicating which block is next to send and receive, respectively.*

a block of data as done, which notifies the Filaments SDSM that it can be sent to the next node in the pipeline. It is asynchronous and called by all nodes except the last. Note the *SDSM* deals with the details of receiving and sending, not the programmer (or compiler). Both functions have a single argument, which is the id of the pipeline. This is actually a *simpler* programming model than the shared-memory program shown in Figure 2.2, because our system keeps the state of the pipeline. Note that none of the complexity of the message-passing model is necessary (no explicit communication of the data arrays no translation of global to local indices is necessary, and no per-node memory allocation). This can be seen be comparing Figures 4.1 and 2.3.

The following section describes the implementation of the one-way pipelining.

4.2.2. Implementation. The one-way pipeline consists of a list of structures, each of which represents a pipeline for a matrix (see Figure 4.2). The list structure of the pipeline provides support for multiple pipelines with different matrices and different block sizes. The pipeline structure itself contains the following information: two counters that specify the block that needs to be sent/received next, a flag vector that tells the node if the block of data has been received, and all the information needed to send/receive the data to/from another node (the start address of the matrix, size of the matrix, and number of blocks). A node that is waiting for a block spins on the corresponding flag, which is set when the message containing the appropriate block is received[1]. The flag vector acts as the synchronization variable for the pipeline. A vector is needed because a node may receive arbitrarily many blocks of data before it completes the computation on the current block; each block must be separately accounted for. Each pipeline is associated with a single matrix and is indexed sequentially by an id in the list of pipelines. A call to `InitPipeline`, described above, creates a pipeline and appends it to the list. The arguments, with the

---

[1]In multithreaded programs, which Filaments supports, spin waiting can be inefficient. However, multithreading is used to overlap communication and computation, which is typically done *without* multithreading in pipelined programs. If a pipelined program also uses multithreading, a blocking synchronization primitive such as a semaphore would need to be used.

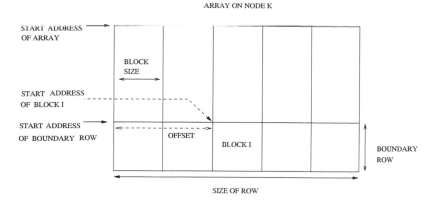

FIG. 4.3. *Block address calculation.*

exception of the id, are used in sending and receiving data.

Function `BlockWait` spins on the flag for the block of data that the node is waiting for from the preceding node. The argument passed to this function is the id of the pipeline associated with the matrix. The flag is reset when the block of data arrives from the node that completed the computation on that block.

Function `BlockDone` causes the Filaments SDSM to send the block whose computation was just completed to the node below, along with the block number and pipeline id. To determine the precise data to send, the address of the start of the block has to be calculated before sending the data, and is done as follows (see Figure 4.3): the page number of the last row is first computed using the start address of the matrix and its size. The address of this page is obtained from the page table. The offset of the block within the last row is calculated using the block number and the size of the block. The start address of the block is then calculated by adding the block offset to the start address of the last row's page.

An incoming message containing a block of data is processed by a specialized handler function, which reads in the message and, using the id of the pipeline stored in the header of the incoming message, traverses the list of pipelines to obtain the pointer to the correct pipeline. The start address of the block that has been received is calculated in the same manner as the `BlockDone` function described above. The data is then copied into the correct address and the flag for that block is reset, allowing the node to begin the computation.

Improvements. In order to extend the pipeline to handle dependencies on rows above *and* below (the example presented in Chapter 2 had only an upward dependence), we actually provide four API functions on blocks: `BlockWaitAbove`, `BlockDoneBelow`, `BlockWaitBelow`, and `BlockDoneAbove`. The first two are the functions described earlier as `BlockWait` and `BlockDone`. Function `Block WaitBelow` is the same as `BlockWaitAbove`, except that it waits on blocks from nodes below. Function `BlockDoneAbove` is the same as `BlockDoneBelow`, except that the SDSM is informed to send boundary data up. Further, the pipeline-invalidate PCP had to be modified to support the bidirectional pipeline by marking the first as well as the last row of each matrix as `READ/WRITE`. Finally, we add a separate send and receive counter, as well as a separate flag vector.

In a number of applications (including ADI integration), more than one matrix is involved in the computation within the same loop(s). In such cases, creating a pipeline for each matrix will cause additional overhead due to an increase in the number of messages sent and received. To decrease this overhead, we improved the implementation so that each pipeline could handle more than one matrix. This means that each message sent contains data from more than one matrix. We implemented a scatter/gather approach that packs one block of data from each of the matrices in the pipeline into one message. On reception of the message, the receiving node unpacks the data and copies the data block of each matrix into the correct location. This approach significantly reduces the number of messages sent and received when multiple matrices are involved in the computation. The following section describes the second approach to adding support for pipelined programs, which is *distributed locks*.

4.3. Distributed Locks.

4.3.1. User Interface.
The Filaments API for Distributed Locks provides the user with three functions that can be used to pipeline the computation: `CreateLock`, `LockAcquire`, and `LockRelease`. The `CreateLock` function enables the user to create a lock and associate it with a block of data to protect. The arguments passed to this function are:

- the id of the lock
- the size and start address of the block of data associated with it
- the owner of the data

Functions `LockAcquire` and `LockRelease` take a single parameter, which is the lock id. A call to `LockAcquire` function attempts to acquire a lock. If the lock is held by another node, the node blocks, waiting for the lock to be released. The `LockRelease` function releases the lock held by a node so that it can be acquired by other nodes requesting it.

4.3.2. Implementation.
The lock-based approach is built on a `request` `/reply` structure as opposed to the one-way pipeline, which employs unidirectional communication. With the lock-based approach, each node has to acquire a lock before it can begin the computation on a block of data. The node releases the lock once it is done with the computation.

However, the locks that we implemented are different from conventional locks in that each lock is bound to the data that it protects (see Figure 4.4). As described above, this is an idea borrowed from the Midway SDSM system [ZSB94] (see also Section 2 for more information) and is essential for better performance because the data is distributed. If the lock and the data are not associated, separate messages for acquiring the lock and faulting on the data

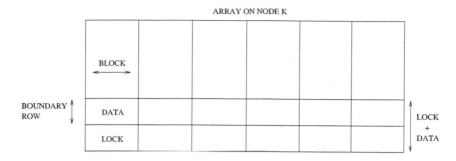

FIG. 4.4. *Distributed lock structure. Note the data is bound to the lock.*

would be required. By binding the lock to the data it protects, a node that acquires the lock will acquire the associated data in the same message.

The implementation of our distributed locks is identical to that described in Midway, so we will not discuss it further here.

4.4. Integration with a Compiler. The SDSM system described in this paper is designed to be the target of a parallelizing compiler. Section 2 discusses related work in integrated compiler/SDSM systems. Our overall goal is to automatically generate efficient, adaptive SDSM code from the SUIF compiler [HAA+96]. We have previously implemented a system called SUIF-Adapt [HL00] that compiles sequential source code into SDSM code, where the data distribution is chosen dynamically for each computational phase in the program.

One limitation of SUIF-Adapt system is that it does not support phases that contain data dependencies. Moreover, SUIF itself does not generate pipelined code when compiling a program like ADI integration. This is because SUIF targets shared-memory multiprocessors, and each directional sweep can be parallelized with no explicit communication. Because our target machine is a multicomputer, a complete data reorganization (transpose) would be necessary, which is a poor way to implement programs like ADI (see Section 5). Hence, we have modified SUIF to generate SDSM code using one-way pipelines. The primary technique is to leverage the dependence analysis already performed by SUIF. The existing analysis marks each loop as either DOALL or DOACROSS. When a loop nest contains an outer DOACROSS and an inner DOALL, SUIF interchanges the loops (when legal) and parallelizes. In current work we have modified the compiler to instead generate pipelined code, similar to that in Figure 4.1 [ML00].

5. Performance. This section presents the performance of six programs. Jacobi iteration, matrix multiplication, and LU decomposition have at least an inner loop that has no data dependencies and hence are explicitly parallel. They give an idea of the performance of our software distributed shared memory (SDSM) system as well as demonstrate that adding the pipeline abstraction does not hurt performance of non-pipelined applications. The other three programs, ADI integration ("ADI"), an implicit hydrodynamics kernel ("Hydro"), and Gauss-Seidel iteration ("GS") contain data dependencies and require pipelining; they test the new features of our SDSM. For these two programs, we experimentally determine an effective block size, present experiments using one-way pipelining and compare to the equivalent programs using distributed locks. Next, for ADI, we present a hand-coded, explicit message passing program for comparison with our system. Finally, we also present performance of an explicit array transpose and show that for ADI, Hydro, and GS, pipelining is a superior solution.

5.1. Experimental Environment. Our experiments were run on a network of Pentium Pro workstations connected by a dedicated 100 Mbps Fast Ethernet. Each workstation has a 200 MHz processor running Solaris, a 64K mixed instruction and data cache, and 64 megabytes of main memory. The network is isolated so that no outside network traffic interferes with the executing programs. Each test was run at least three times and the reported result is the median. All tests were compiled with `cc -O`.

5.2. Non-Pipelined Applications. We experimented with three non-pipelined applications: Jacobi iteration, matrix multiplication, and LU Decomposition. Jacobi iteration can be used to solve Laplace's equation, $\frac{\partial^2 u}{\partial x^2} + \frac{\partial^2 u}{\partial y^2} = 0$, in two dimensions. Matrix multiplication computes the matrix product $C = AB$. Both use a block assignment of rows to nodes. LU decomposition is used to solve the linear system $Ax = b$. On each iteration, the workload decreases; hence, a cyclic assignment of rows to nodes is used to balance the load. Short code fragments for each of these programs are shown in Figure 5.1. All three use the write-invalidate page consistency protocol, *not* the pipeline-invalidate protocol.

Figure 5.2 shows the performance of these three applications. Execution time is broken down into at most five categories:

- Initialization. This is the time to perform (implicitly) the initial data distribution. This component consists of page faulting and servicing, but is accounted separately to give an idea of the time taken for page traffic *on each iteration*.
- Computation. This is the time actually spent performing the computation.
- Page fault time. This is the time (outside of initialization) a node spends faulting, sending requests, and receiving replies.
- Page servicing time. This is the time (outside of initialization) a node spends servicing other nodes' page faults (i.e., sending replies).
- Barrier synchronization. This is the time spent to perform global synchronization across all nodes (typically done after each iteration).

Matrix multiplication and LU decomposition only incur faults in initialization; furthermore, matrix multiplication is not iterative and hence has no barriers (other than one at the end of the computation).

All three applications achieve speedup on two, four, and eight nodes. Jacobi iteration incurs page sharing between a node and its two neighbors (the first and last nodes are special cases). Still, the paging time is relatively small, because

```
Jacobi iteration

while not done
  for (i = startrow to endrow)
    for (j = 1 to n)
      A[i][j] = (B[i+1][j] + B[i+1][j] + B[i][j+1] + B[i][j-1])/4
  synchronize; check for termination

Matrix Multiplication

for (i = startrow to endrow)
  for (j = 1 to n)
    sum = 0
    for (k = 1 to n)
      sum += A[i][k] * B[k][j]
    C[i][j] = sum

LU Decomposition

for (k = 1 to n)
  for (i = k+startrow to endrow by numNodes)
    for (j = k+1 to n)
      A[i][j] = A[i][j] - A[k][j] * A[i][k];

Hydro

for iter := 1 to NUMITERS
  for jj := 0 to N-1 by blocksize
    if (myId != 0)
      BlockWait(1);  /* parameter is pipeline id */
    for i := start to end
      for j := jj to jj+blocksize-1
        A[i][j] := A[i][j] + A[i][j+1]*B[i][j] + A[i][j-1]*B[i][j] +
                   A[i+1][j]*C[i][j] + A[i-1][j]*C[i][j] + D[i][j];
    if (myId != p-1)
      BlockDone(1);  /* parameter is pipeline id */

GS

for iter := 1 to NUMITERS
  for jj := 0 to N-1 by blocksize
    if (myId != 0)
      BlockWait(1);  /* parameter is pipeline id */
    for i := start to end
      for j := jj to jj+blocksize-1
        A[i][j] = (A[i+1][j] + A[i+1][j] + A[i][j+1] + A[i][j-1])/4
    if (myId != p-1)
      BlockDone(1);  /* parameter is pipeline id */
```

FIG. 5.1. *Outlines of the key parts of five test programs. The first three, Jacobi iteration, matrix multiplication, and LU decomposition, do not require pipelining. The last two, Hydro and GS, do. Variables startrow and endrow are each node's first and last row.*

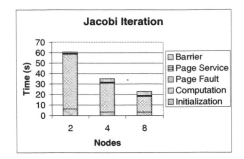

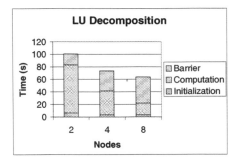

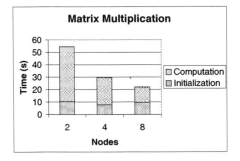

FIG. 5.2. *Performance of non-pipelined applications (Jacobi iteration, LU decomposition, and matrix multiplication). Times are given in seconds. Problem sizes were 1024 for Jacobi, 1400 for LU, and 1024 for matrix multiplication. Sequential times were 99, 190, and 112 seconds, respectively.*

there is a significant amount of computation. LU decomposition tails off at eight nodes; this is because there are two barrier synchronizations per iteration and the amount of work decreases on each iteration. Finally, matrix multiplication achieves good speedup, as there is relatively little communication.

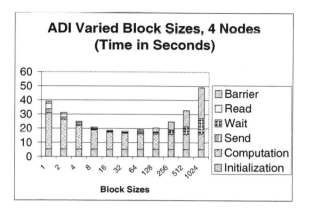

FIG. 5.3. *Times for each (power of two) block size for ADI using a matrix size of 1024 and four nodes. The times reported are from the second node (id 1). A smaller block size has more communication overhead (and often increased computation time; see text), and a larger block size has more wait time. Mid-range block sizes (16, 32, 64) serve as effective compromises.*

It is important to note that because these programs use the regular write-invalidate page consistency protocol, there is no extra overhead that might be incurred due to the pipeline-invalidate protocol (see below). For example, there are no explicit messages sent between nodes (as is necessary in pipelined programs). Hence, our integration of pipelining support in our SDSM does not affect non-pipelined applications.

5.3. Pipelined Applications. We now focus on our three pipelined applications, ADI, Hydro, and GS. These programs use the pipeline-invalidate protocol; code fragments are shown in Figure 4.1 (ADI) and in Figure 5.1 (Hydro, GS). Note that for pipelined applications, actions performed by nodes are not uniform. For example, the first node (id 0) in the pipeline does not receive, and the last node (id $P-1$) does not send. Hence, all time breakdowns given are from the second node (id 1), which sends *and* receives, although its wait time will be smaller than nodes 2 through $P-1$.

Determining Block Size. Figure 5.3 shows a range of times for ADI integration using an array of size 1024 and block sizes of 1-1024, with a data point at each power of two. The time is broken down in the same way as the last section, with the addition of three categories:

- Send. This is the time spent copying the message to the kernel in preparation for sending.
- Wait. This is the time a node is blocked waiting for data.
- Read. This is the time spent copying the message from the kernel into

the user buffer. Note that messages may arrive prior to their use; for such messages, the wait time will be zero.

For ADI integration (as well as the implicit hydrodynamics kernel and Gauss-Seidel iteration, which are discussed below), all paging traffic occurs in initialization.

The block size in pipelined code has a crucial effect on performance. The larger the block size, the smaller the number of messages sent over the network; however, the latency increases. This can be seen upon inspection of the larger block sizes (256, 512, 1024). Note that a block size of 1024 sequentializes the computation. With small block sizes (e.g. 1, 2, and 4), there are several overheads. First, more messages are sent and received, so the communication overhead causes the performance to degrade. Furthermore, smaller block sizes make ineffective use of the cache, because columns are traversed instead of rows [Low00]. In addition, the receipt of messages interrupts computation [VSM96]. The combination of these two things explains the larger computation time on smaller block sizes. For ADI integration (as well as Hydro), a block size of 32 was experimentally determined to be the most effective (out of all powers of two). For Gauss-Seidel iteration, the best size was 64. This is because there is a smaller amount of work per point than in the other two programs.

Choosing an effective block size is a difficult problem. As discussed at the end of Section 2, we have developed a run-time system for use with message passing programs that chooses an effective block size by monitoring the program for a single iteration. That work is orthogonal to the work described in this paper; here, we focus on the infrastructure necessary to enable pipelining in SDSM systems.

Performance of One-Way Pipeline and Distributed Locks. Figure 5.4 shows the timing results for ADI integration Hydro, and GS, using both one-way pipelining and distributed locks. They show that the one-way pipeline generally allows good speedup. The speedups on eight nodes for ADI, Hydro, and GS, respectively, are 5, 4.3, and 2.3. However, the speedup when using distributed locks is significantly less, achieving 4 on eight nodes for ADI, 2.9 for Hydro, and 1.7 for GS. The speedup is much lower for GS because there is an extremely small amount of work (just four additions and a division), and a relatively large amount of (pipelined) communication. This manifests itself in very large barrier synchronization times.

There are two primary sources of overhead in the lock-based programs compared to the one-way pipelined ones. First, waiting time is increased because of the request/reply structure of locks; each node has to first send out a message to acquire the lock and data. On the other hand, the one-way pipeline has no request messages; each node instead blocks until the data is received from the preceding node. One might think that the extra messages in the lock-based program do not contribute to the overhead since they are just requests and carry no data. However, we found by experimentation that there is little difference in sending an empty message compared to sending a message with a small amount

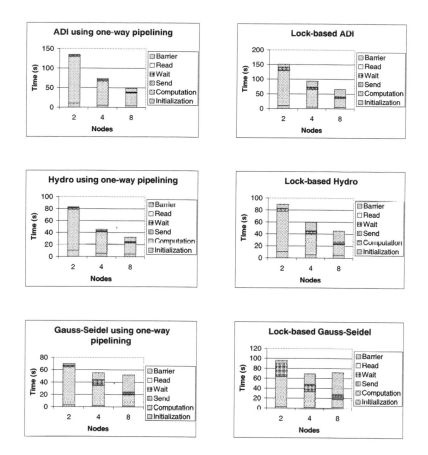

FIG. 5.4. *Performance of one-way pipelining and lock-based versions of ADI, Hydro, and GS. A block size of 32 was used for the first two, and a block size of 64 was used for GS. The sequential times were 239 seconds for ADI, 137 seconds for Hydro, and 119 seconds for GS. ADI and Hydro were run for 100 iterations, and GS was run for 300 iterations. All times reported are from the second node (id 1).*

of data.

More importantly, after each iteration, all locks must be re-acquired by the node that owned them at the start of the iteration. For example, if a block size of 32 is used with a matrix size of 1024, 32 locks (one per block) must be acquired by each node (except the last one). This presents a significant overhead. Note that one might argue that the locks can simply be implicitly reset, which avoids communication. However, that is really one-way pipelining; in a true lock-based program, the lock must be re-acquired.

One-Way Pipelining vs. Message Passing. For comparison, the results of the explicit message-passing ADI program (which was outlined in Figure 2.3)

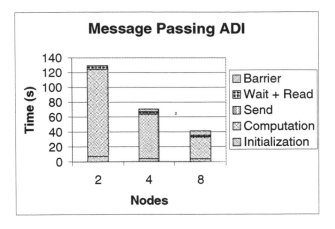

FIG. 5.5. *Times for explicit message passing version of ADI integration, size 1024. The sequential time is 239 seconds. All times reported are from the second node (id 1). The wait and read times are combined in this figure, because the socket library did not allow us to obtain the times separately.*

TABLE 5.1
Timing results of SDSM transpose for an array of size 1024. Also shown are the per-iteration times for ADI, Hydro, and GS. All times are in seconds.

Nodes	Array Size	Transpose	ADI (1 iter)	Hydro (1 iter)	GS (1 iter)
2	1024	4.49	1.23	0.74	0.22
4	1024	3.72	0.67	0.40	0.18
8	1024	4.26	0.42	0.28	0.17

with size 1024 are shown in Figure 5.5. This hand-coded program uses sockets for communication instead of using the SDSM; otherwise the programs are the same. It shows that the one-way pipeline program is competitive; in the worst case, it is 17% slower than the message passing program. The differences show up in the the initialization time as well as in the barrier synchronization code. The former will always be slower, because explicit (send/receive) messages are faster than implicit (page fault-based) messages. We believe that the barrier synchronization code takes longer due to a higher variance between nodes in the one-way pipelining version. (for example, in one-way pipelining we must send explicit acknowledgments). It should be kept in mind that the one-way pipeline program is written with a shared-memory model, and so a slight degradation in performance compared to an explicit message-passing program is expected.

Transpose. As we discussed in Chapter 2, an alternate solution to pipelining in some problems is to perform each phase in parallel without any communication, with a transpose in between the two phases. However, computing the transpose of a distributed matrix is an expensive operation because it involves all to all communication between the nodes. To illustrate this, we present the timing results we obtained for a SDSM transpose of matrices of different sizes in Table 5.1. We found that the times taken for a single SDSM transpose are greater than the time taken by the pipelined versions of the ADI, Hydro, and GS programs for 1 iteration, which are also shown.

In addition, we will have to compute the transpose twice in an application such as the one in Section 2 (to return the matrix to its original state). From the data presented in Table 5.1, it is obvious that the SDSM transpose is a much less efficient solution than the pipeline. For example, on the two-node ADI program, we find that the pipelined program takes 1.23 seconds per iteration. The SDSM transpose takes 4.29 seconds for a matrix of the same size. Because two transposes will be required per iteration, we find that the transpose needs to be at least eight times faster for it to compete with the performance of the pipelining for these applications. Note that one could write an explicit message-passing transpose; however, it is difficult to implement. Furthermore, it is not likely provide a eight-fold improvement (we tried one efficient algorithm, and it was no more than twice as fast). Hence, for our applications, pipelining the computation provides a more efficient solution than a transpose-based solution.

6. Conclusion. This paper discusses the issues involved in the implementation of efficient pipelining in software distributed shared memory (SDSM) systems. We have presented the design and implementation of both one-way pipelining and distributed locks as extensions to Filaments, a software kernel that provides a SDSM. While both extensions were implemented in Filaments, they are general in the sense that they could be added to any standard SDSM system.

We showed that one-way pipelining is the superior solution because it sends close to the minimal amount of data—in fact, it sends almost the same amount of data one would send in an equivalent program that uses message passing. For this reason, one-way pipelining is very competitive with explicit message-passing programs; the former was always within 17% of the latter in ADI integration experiments. Furthermore, we showed that one-way pipelining is far superior to using an explicit transpose. Indeed, our implementation of one-way pipelining increases the number of applications that can be efficiently supported by SDSM systems.

REFERENCES

[AK87]   J.R. Allen and K. Kennedy. Automatic translation of Fortran programs to vector form. *TOPLAS*, 9(4).491–542, October 1987.

[BCG+95]   P. Banerjee, J.A. Chandy, M. Gupta, E.W. Hodges IV, J.G. Holm, A. Lain, D.J. Palermo, S. Ramaswamy, and E. Su. The PARADIGM compiler for

120   Karthik Balasubramanian and David K. Lowenthal

distributed-memory multicomputers. *IEEE Computer*, 28(10):37–47, October 1995.

[BZS93]   Brian N. Bershad, Matthew J. Zekauskas, and Wayne A. Sawdon. The Midway distributed shared memory system. In *COMPCON '93*, pages 528–537, 1993.

[CBZ91]   John B. Carter, John K. Bennett, and Willy Zwaenepoel. Implementation and performance of Munin. In *Proceedings of 13th ACM Symposium On Operating Systems*, pages 152–164, October 1991.

[CDLZ97]   Alan L. Cox, Sandhya Dwarkadus, Honghui Lu, and Willy Zwanapoel. Evaluating the performance of software distributed shared memory as a target for parallelizing compilers. In *Proceedings of the 11th International Parallel Processing Symposium*, pages 474–482, April 1997.

[CM00]   Daniel Chavarria-Miranda and John Mellor-Crummey. Towards compiler support for scalable parallelism. In *Fifth Workshop on Languages, Compilers, and Run-Time Systems for Scalable Computers*, May 2000.

[FA96]   Vincent W. Freeh and Gregory R. Andrews. Dynamically controlling false sharing in distributed shared memory. In *Proceedings of the 5th Symposium on High Performance Distributed Computing*, August 1996.

[FLA94]   Vincent W. Freeh, David K. Lowenthal, and Gregory R. Andrews. Distributed Filaments: Efficient fine-grain parallelism on a cluster of workstations. In *First Symposium on Operating Systems Design and Implementation*, pages 201–212, November 1994.

[HAA+96]   Mary W. Hall, Jennifer M. Anderson, Saman P. Amarasinghe, Brian R. Murphy, Shih-Wei Liao, Edouard Bugnion, and Monica S. Lam. Maximizing multiprocessor performance with the SUIF compiler. *IEEE Computer*, 29(12):84–89, December 1996.

[HL00]   Gregory M.S. Howard and David K. Lowenthal. An integrated compiler/runtime system for global data distribution in distributed shared memory systems. In *Second Workshop on Software Distributed Shared Memory*, May 2000.

[HLKL97]   A.R. Hurson, Joford T. Lim, Krishna M. Kavi, and Ben Lee. *Parallelization of DOALL and DOACROSS Loops — A Survey*, volume 45, pages 53–103. Academic Press Ltd., 1997.

[HYW+00]   Y. Charlie Hu, Weimin Yu, Dan Wallach, Alan Cox, and Willy Zwaenepoel. Runtime support for distributed sharing in typed languages. In *Fifth Workshop on Languages, Compilers, and Run-Time Systems for Scalable Computers*, pages 89–95, May 2000.

[ID98]   Sotiris Ioannidis and Sandhya Dwarkadas. Compiler and run-time support for adaptive load balancing in software distributed shared memory systems. In *Proceedings of the Fourth Workshop on Languages, Compilers, and Run-Time Systems for Parallel Computing*, pages 107–122, May 1998.

[IDFL96]   Liviu Iftode, C Dubnicki, Ed Felton, and Kai Li. Improving release-consistent shared virtual memory using automatic update. In *Proceedings of the 2nd IEEE Symposium on High-Performance Computer Architecture*, February 1996.

[Ift98]   Liviu Iftode. *Home-Based Shared Virtual Memory*. PhD thesis, Princeton University, June 1998.

[IPL96]   Liviu Iftode, Jaswinder Pal Singh, and Kai Li. Scope consistency: a bridge between release consistency and entry consistency. In *Proceedings of the 8th Annual ACM Symposium on Parallel Algorithms and Architectures*, June 1996.

[IS99]   A. Itzkovitz and A. Schuster. Multiview and Millipage – fine-grain sharing in page-based dsms. In *Proceedings of the Third Symposium on Operating Systems Design and Implementation*, February 1999.

[KDCZ94]   Pete Keleher, Sandhya Dwarkadas, Alan Cox, and Willy Zwaenepoel. TreadMarks: Distributed shared memory on standard workstations and operating systems. In *Proceedings of the 1994 Winter Usenix Conference*, pages 115–

131, January 1994.

[KF94]   Povl T. Koch and Robert J. Fowler. Integrating message-passing with lazy release consistent distributed shared memory. In *First Operating Systems Design and Implementation*, November 1994.

[KT97]   Pete Keleher and Chau-Wen Tseng. Enhancing software DSM for compiler-parallelized applications. In *Proceedings of the 11th International Parallel Processing Symposium*, April 1997.

[KTG95]   V.P. Krothapalli, J. Thulasiraman, and M. Giesbrecht. Run-time parallelization of irregular DOACROSS loops. In *Proceedings of Irregular '95*, pages 75–80, 1995.

[LCD+97]   Honghui Lu, Alan L. Cox, Sandhya Dwarkadas, Ramakrishnan Rajamony, and Willy Zwaenepoel. Compiler and distributed shared memory support for irregular applications. In *Sixth ACM SIGPLAN Symposium on Principles and Practice of Parallel Programming*, pages 48–56, June 1997.

[LDCZ95]   Honghui Lu, Sandhya Dwarkadas, Alan L. Cox, and Willy Zwaenepoel. Message passing versus distributed shared memory on networks of workstations. In *Supercomputing '95*, December 1995.

[LFA96]   David K. Lowenthal, Vincent W. Freeh, and Gregory R. Andrews. Using fine-grain threads and run-time decision making in parallel computing. *Journal of Parallel and Distributed Computing*, 37:41–54, November 1996.

[LH89]   Kai Li and Paul Hudak. Memory coherence in shared virtual memory systems. *ACM Transactions on Computer Systems*, 7(4), November 1989.

[LJ99]   David K. Lowenthal and Michael James. Run-time selection of block size in pipelined parallel programs. In *Proceedings of the 2nd Merged IPPS/SPDP*, pages 82–87, April 1999.

[Lov77]   D.B. Loveman. Program improvement by source-to-source transformation. *Journal of the ACM*, 24(1):129–138, January 1977.

[Low00]   David K. Lowenthal. Accurately selecting block size at run-time in pipelined parallel programs. *International Journal of Parallel Programming*, 28(3):245–274, 2000.

[ML00]   Donald G. Morris and David K. Lowenthal. Compiling pipelined computations for distributed shared memory systems (in preparation). July 2000.

[Mos93]   David Mosberger. Memory consistency models. *Operating Systems Review*, 27(1):18–26, January 1993.

[RCJM99]   Sumit Roy, Vipin Choudhary, Shi Jia, and Padmanabhan Menon. Application based evaluation of distributed shared memory versus message passing. In *Proceedings of ISCA 12th Intl. Conference on Parallel and Distributed Computing Systems*, August 1999.

[Tse93]   Chau-Wen Tseng. *An Optimizing Fortran D Compiler for MIMD Distributed-Memory Machines*. PhD thesis, Rice University, January 1993.

[VSM96]   Rob F. Van der Wijngaart, Sekhar R. Sarukkai, and Pankaj Mehra. The effect of interrupts on software pipeline execution on message-passing architectures. In *Proceedings of ACM Int'l. Conference on Supercomputing*, May 1996.

[ZSB94]   Matthew J. Zekauskas, Wayne A. Sawdon, and Brian N. Bershad. Software write detection for distributed shared memory. In *First Operating Systems Design and Implementation*, November 1994.

THE ESTIMATION OF THE WCET IN SUPER-SCALAR REAL-TIME SYSTEM

HASSAN ALJIFRI *, ALEXANDER PONS *, AND MOIEZ TAPIA§

Abstract. Predicting and estimating the execution time of a program is of the utmost importance to designers of real-time systems, particularly hard real-time systems. This paper describes an algorithm for estimating an improved WCET (worst-case execution time) of a real-time program that utilizes a path generating approach to factor into the calculation the effects of super-scalar processor pipelining. The algorithm starts by determining the program's control flow. The pipelining analysis takes into account the simultaneous execution of instructions in distinct blocks in two separate pipelines. The timing tool uses the pipelining analysis to estimate the WCET. The results indicate that this method enhances the acquisition of tighter estimates.

Key words. real-time, WCET, program-path, program-tree, program-cover, pipeline.

1. Introduction. Thousands of electrical, electronic, mechanical, aeronautical, biomedical and other types of devices have microprocessors embedded in them. These systems belong to the class of hard real-time systems. A hard real-time system is one that must satisfy explicit bounded response time constraints. Failure to do so may result in the failure of the system. In real-time, even in the worst case, a task must be processed and completed before its deadline. There have been various scheduling techniques developed to ensure that tasks meet their deadline. As a requirement, these techniques must have the worst-case execution time of each task apriori [1]. For this purpose, a tremendous amount of research has concentrated on the estimation of the worst-case execution time [WCET] of tasks. In essence, the purpose of this paper is to propose a method for predicting the time behavior of high-level programs, using assembly code. The method will help determine whether a program will execute under its timing constraints. Providing accurate analysis for developers will aid in program correctness. Furthermore, an accurate and automated analysis is less time consuming, complicated and prone to error than manual analysis.

Many researchers [2] [3] [4] [5] [6] [7] [8] [9] [10] [11] have studied and proposed methods of solution for estimating the execution time of real time software. Some of them have addressed the effect of a single pipeline on the execution time of a real-time system [2] [7] [8] [11]. To obtain accurate prediction for modern high-performance processors, the timing effect of advanced architectural features should be taken into account. Most of the existing techniques assume that processors can issue at most one instruction at each cycle. Hence they cannot produce accurate analysis results for super-scalar processor [12]. Choi, Lee and Kang [13] and Harcourt, Mauney and Cock [14] have proposed a method to estimate the WCET of a pipelined processor. Although these methods have the advantages of being formal and machine independent, their applications are

---

*Computer Information Systems, University of Miami, Coral Gables, FL
§Electrical and Computer Engineering, University of Miami, Coral Gables, FL

limited to calculating the execution time of a sequence of instructions or a given sequence of basic blocks.

In super-scalar processor the amount of exploiting parallelism is restricted by dependencies among instruction and by the order in which the instructions are issued since, in some super-scalar processors (i.e. Pentium), not all the instructions can be executed in any pipeline and the parallelism depends on which instruction is executed in which pipeline. In this paper, we propose a worst-case timing estimation algorithm, which is applicable to processors that issue different instruction to different pipelines. The proposed algorithm is not intended to target a specific processor, but instead a class of processors with dual pipelines similar to Pentium. However, we will use the Pentium processors as a case study to show the validity of our algorithm.

2. Steps to a Tight Estimation. The approach to finding the WCET of a program is to know the path the program will take during execution. Since a program can take only one of a finite number of paths, the paths have to be constructed and tested. To construct the program's path, one needs to know what segment(s) of assembly code constitute(s) each path. In order to know this, a program's assembly code has to be divided into blocks. A given block may belong to more than one path. We will divide the whole program into blocks. Then we will construct a tree graph for the assembly code given by a compiler. From this tree, we will obtain a Program Paths Cover, PPC, to be defined later in section §4. Finally, using PPC, a list of the possible paths is generated and the time of each path that the program might take during execution is computed.

Consider a super-scalar processor, Pentium for example, with two pipelines U and V. When two instructions appear together in a program and have no data dependency, they can be executed simultaneously by placing one of them in pipeline U and the other in pipeline V. When two instructions are thus placed simultaneously in the two pipelines, they are said to be paired. The classification of the instructions assumes the Pentium processor and is based on whether they can be paired or not and how they can be paired if they are pairable. A similar classification would be needed for a different super-scalar processor.

1. Class NP: This is a set of unpairable instructions. Long arithmetic instructions *mul* and *div* belong to this class.

2. Class UV: This is a class of pairable instructions that may either go to U or V pipe.

3. Class PU: This is a class of pairable instructions that could be paired only if they are issued to the U pipeline. Instructions to shift and rotate and instructions *adc* and *sbb* can be placed only in the U pipe to be paired.

4. Class PV: This is a class of pairable instructions that could be paired only if they are issued to the V pipeline. Instructions *jmp*, call and *jcc* belong to this class.

Instructions cannot be paired due to register contention. Register contention is a conflict over the use of a register due to data dependencies between two instructions. Register contention prevents two instructions from pairing. Register

TABLE 2.1
Example of blocks overlapping.

Block Number	Instruction-Type	Number of Cycles
0	PU	1
1	PV	1
1	PU	1
2	PV	1
2	PU	1
3	PV	1
3	PU	1

contention may be caused by flow-dependency, or by output-dependency. Flow-dependency is when the first instruction writes to a register and the second instruction reads from the same register. Consider the following instruction:

add eax, 9

add [ebp],eax

The destination in the first instruction is the source in the second instruction. The source data for the second instruction is available only after the first instruction has been executed. Hence these two instructions cannot be executed in parallel in two distinct pipelines. When both instructions write to the same register, we say there is output-dependency between them. The following example illustrates output-dependency:

add eax,9

add eax,[ebp]

If an instruction cannot be paired (Due to its classification or register contention with another instruction), it must be executed in the U pipeline. Therefore, the pairing process and the WCET depends on the instructions execution order. If the algorithm calculates the WCET of each atomic block independently and not taking into account the overlapping of blocks, it would lead to not only a pessimistic result but to a significant deviation from the actual WCET resulting in severe under-utilization of machine resources. When considering only a code block rather than the entire program (in pipeline), miscalculation of the WCET would result. This is due to the fact that the execution time of the processor's instructions at the block junction may depend on their pairability, the instructions being in distinct blocks.

Consider the sequence of instructions in Table 2.1. Assume that each block is executed independently.

In the Table 2.1, there are four independent blocks. There is no pairing between the instructions within block number n, $1 \leq n \leq 3$, because the starting instruction of the block number n is a PV instruction. This means that the first instruction in all of the blocks 1, 2 and 3 can be paired only if it is placed in the V pipeline. However, since it is the first instruction in the block, it will have to go to the U pipeline in order for it to be paired with the following instruction. When the second instruction comes, it will find that the U pipeline is full and therefore it cannot be paired because in order for it to be paired it will have to go to the U pipeline. Therefore, it will wait until the first instruction finishes and then it will execute in the U pipeline. The overall clock cycles that the above blocks will take to execute are seven cycles. Now consider overlapping of instructions between blocks. The instruction in the block n, $n = 0, 1, 2$, will go to the U pipeline, and the first instruction of block $(n + 1)$ will go to the V pipeline. Their simultaneous execution takes only one clock cycle. The overall clock cycles that the above blocks will take are four cycles. This demonstrates that taking the overlapping of blocks into account could improve the WCET of a program.

2.1. Partitioning a Program into Blocks. In what follows, it will be assumed that a program being analyzed is a program in Pentium assembly language code. To facilitate generation of distinct paths in the program, we will decompose it into blocks as described below:

DEFINITION 2.1. *A block or node in a program is a contiguous segment of the program or sequence of instructions in the program that is being analyzed.*

DEFINITION 2.2. *cmp, jcc, jmp and test will be called intra-transfer instructions. Call and ret will be called inter-transfer instructions. Intra-transfer and inter-transfer instructions will be called transfer instructions.*

DEFINITION 2.3. *A serial block is the largest possible sequence of instructions in a program that includes no transfer instructions.*

DEFINITION 2.4. *Each one of the following blocks is an atomic or a basic block:*

- *a block comprising just one of the inter-transfer instructions,*
- *a block of sequence of instructions, in the program, obtained by adding cmp, jcc or test instruction to a serial block that immediately follows, in the program, cmp, jcc or test instruction, respectively,*
- *a block of sequence of instructions in the program obtained by adding the sequence pair (cmp, jcc) or (test, jcc) to a serial block that immediately follows, in the program, (cmp, jcc) or (test, jcc) sequence pair, respectively,*
- *a block comprising the entire program if it does not have any transfer instruction in it, and*
- *each one of the two blocks that a serial block that immediately precedes, in the program, jmp instruction gives rise to in the following way: one block is formed by adding the jmp instruction to the portion of the serial block between and including the instruction that jmp instruction jumps back to, and the other block is the rest of the serial block.*

2.2. Algorithm for generation of blocks. In Order to generate blocks, we will generate Level-s blocks as described below;

- Let i, $(i \geq 1)$, denote the ith position of the instruction in the program and $B[s, m]$ denote the mth block at the sth level in the program, $s = 1$ and $m = 1$.
- $i = 1$, $s = 1$ and $m = 1$. As we can scan the program, let i^{th} string be the 'current' instruction being scanned and $B[s, m]$ be the current block

being generated.

- If the ith instruction is not a transfer instruction, place it in block $B[s, m]$.
- If the ith instruction is an intra-transfer instruction cmp, jcc or test, then it will be included at the beginning of the 'next' block $B[s, m+1]$ that is to be created , respectively. $B[s, m+1]$ will contain all the instructions up to but not including the instruction which has a starting address equal to the operand of the jcc. In case of jcc, the target address in the jcc instruction will be the address of the instruction at the beginning of a new block$B[s, m+2]$.
- If the ith instruction is an inter-transfer instruction call or ret, then it will be included in a one instruction block by itself, $B[s, m+1]$. The next i^{th} instruction will start in block $B[s, m+2]$.
- If the ith instruction is an intra-transfer instruction jmp or loop, then all the previous instructions up to and including the jmp or loop will be included at the end in the 'current' block $B[s, m]$.
- i will be increased if any instruction remained un-scanned. If no more instruction remains to be scanned, i is set to 1 and s will be increased by 1 and all the previous steps for possibly decomposing one or more of $B[s, m]$ blocks will be carried out. The algorithm stops when in a complete pass, no block is decomposed. All the blocks in m^{th} level, m having the largest value for the level of decomposition, are atomic blocks.

2.3. Example on how to generate blocks . Consider the assembly code in Fig. 2.1. Starting at the first line of the program, which is line 00401010, the algorithm scans the op-codes for any of the transfer instruction [$call, cmp, jcc,$ $jmp, ret, test$]. The first one to encounter is cmp at line 0040102B. The algorithm marks the block of assembly code (line 00401010 to line 00401024) before that transfer instruction as block 1. So, line 0040102F become the first line of the second block, and since the op-code is cmp, the next op-code rights after it is jcc. The address line of where the jle should go is 004010A2, which means that the second block ends right before that address. Block number 2 goes from line 0040102B to line 004010A0. Note that the last line of block 2 is a jmp and the jmp to address is 0040102B, which is less than the starting address of that jmp (004010A0) implying that block number 2 is a loop block. The third block starts at address line 004010A2, and the search continues to find the next transfer instruction. The third block ends at line 004010A4, which is the line before the transfer instruction ret. The fourth block is just the ret op-code that is line 004010A5. The algorithm will examine each block starting from the first block until the last one. Choosing block number 1, the algorithm will scan the block, looking for any transfer instructions. Since there are no transfer instructions within block 1, the block is marked as serial block. Moving to block number 2, the algorithm looks for transfer instructions. It finds one at line 00401038. This means that the assembly code before that will be marked as block number 2.1

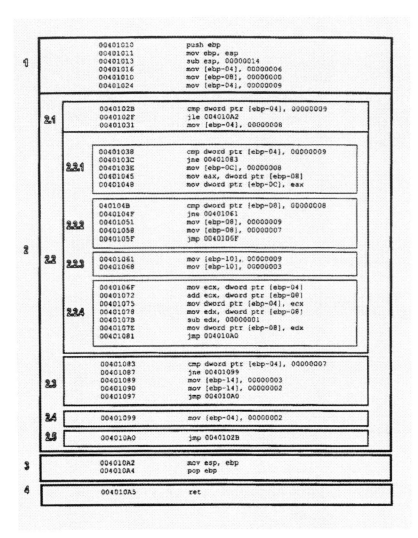

FIG. 2.1. *Example of blocks' generation.*

(line 0040102B to line 00401031). Since the transfer instruction is *cmp*, the last address of the current block (2.2) is the address of the jump of *jcc(jne)*, which is 00401081). So block 2.2 starts at line 00401038 and ends at line: 00401083. Block 2.3 starts at line 00401083. This line contains a *cmp* op-code, which means that the next op-code is a *jcc(jne)*. Block 2.3 ends at the line 00401097, which is right before where the *jne* should jump. Line 00401099 is a block (2.4) by itself because it comes between the end of a block and a transfer instruction (jmp). Line 004010A0 is a transfer instruction line. Therefore, it is a block (2.5) by itself. Again, the algorithm scans all the blocks in ascending order. So, it will have to finish block 3 and 4 before further exploration of blocks 2.1 - 2.5. However, both blocks 3 and 4 are serial and atomic blocks respectively. So block 2.1 is explored next. Block 2.1 itself is an atomic block, which means the next block to explore is block 2.2. Block number 2.2 is scanned. It contains the following blocks 2.2.1, 2.2.2, 2.2.3 and 2.2.4. Block 2.3, 2.5 are atomic blocks and block 2.4 is a serial block. Blocks 2.2.1, 2.2.2 and 2.2.4 are atomic blocks and block 2.2.3 is serial block, which means no further exploration is necessary.

3. Program Tree Graph (PTG). The program tree graph is basically a tree representation of blocks or nodes, where each block or node represents a nested block, except for the leaf node that represents an atomic block. Before proceeding, we need to define loop node (or loop block) and conditional node (or conditional block).

DEFINITION 3.1. *A block is defined as loop block or loop node if it has a jmp instruction at the end of the block and the destination address of this jmp instruction is the starting address of the block.*

The next block to be defined is due to a *jcc* instruction. The flag in this instruction could be affected by a *cmp* instruction or some other instruction prior to this instruction that affects the flag.

DEFINITION 3.2. *An instruction that affects one or more flags relating to the condition of the jcc instruction that follows and is closet to it will be called flag affecting instruction and denoted by FAI.*

DEFINITION 3.3. *If a loop is such that the jmp instruction at the end of it has a target address that is less than that of the FAI instruction in the loop, it will be called a 2-block loop and it will be decomposed at the FAI instruction, the latter being included in the higher-address block.*

DEFINITION 3.4. *A block of instructions is defined as simple or 1-way conditional block if the start of the the block is a cmp instruction or any other instruction that affects the flag specified in the first jcc instruction that comes after it, and the end of the block is the instruction before the target address of the jcc that follows the instruction and it has no conditional or unconditional jump instruction between the jcc instruction and the target address of this instruction.*

DEFINITION 3.5. *A block of instructions is defined as an n-compound or n-way, $n \geq 1$, conditional block or node if we have n jcc instructions and $(n-2)$ jmp instruction occurring*

In order to generate all distinct paths, we will use the following rules:

- The only entry to the Program Path Tree is at the root node.
- A path starts from the root to the rightmost branch of the tree and proceeds to the left,scanning depth wise first, passing through their children.
- A path can be from the right sibling to the left one, not vice versa.

DEFINITION 3.6. *A unique integer number, called local id ≥ 1, will be* *assigned to every component node in every 2-block loop node and in every n-compound conditional block. This local id is the same for all the nodes at the same level in PTG which belong to the same 2-block loop or n-compound conditional node. The two nodes in the 2-block loop group will be given the same local id.*

Consider the assembly code in Fig. 2.1. The tree representation of that code is shown in Fig. 3.1. Note that all the leaf nodes are atomic blocks. The path starts from node 0 and goes right to node 1. Then, it proceeds to node 2 that is a loop node; node 2.1 is the next step. Now, there are three nodes to choose from: 2.2, 2.3 and 2.4; exactly one of them will be selected in a given path. If node 2.2 is chosen, then node 2.2.1 is visited next. Exactly one node will be selected: either node 2.2.2 or 2.2.3. Assume node 2.2.3 is chosen; then node 2.2.4 is visited. This concludes node 2.2. Next we will consider node 2.5 followed, by node 3 and node 4. In Fig. 3.1, C1 indicates a conditional node with local id of 1, and C2 indicates a conditional node with local id of 2.

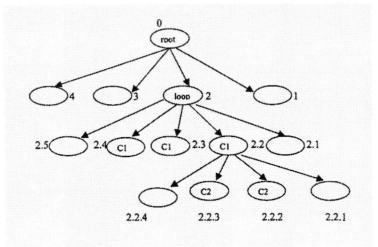

FIG. 3.1. *Tree representation of the code in Fig. 2.1*

4. Program Path Cover (PPC). DEFINITION 4.1. *A set of nodes all of which are executed in a sequence will be called a sequentially executed group and will be enclosed in a pair of angular brackets ' <' and ' >'. The set of nodes enclosed by ' <' and ' >' will be treated as a single node.*

DEFINITION 4.2. *A loop node will be enclosed in a pair of braces '{'and '}'.*

DEFINITION 4.3. *All the n components of an n-compound block will be enclosed in a pair of parentheses '(' and ')'. Exactly one node in this group is executed when the entire program is executed.*

The ith Program Path Cover, PPC_i, i being an integer ≥ 0, is a nonempty sequence of one or more sequentially-executable groups and/or zero or more conditional groups and /or zero or more loop blocks such that these groups correspond to the nodes in the program tree as you scan the tree from right to left, the sequence of these groups in the PPC_i and the sequence of nodes at i^{th} level of the tree being the same.

When the delimiter @ is placed before loop or conditional block n_k , k being an integer ≥ 1, as a prefix to n_k , $@n_k$ represents the subset of n_k which comprises only sequence of instructions in n_k which test whether iteration should be continued or exited if it is a loop, and which test if a jump should occur or not if it is a conditional node.

During the process of generating the PPC for a program, we will check every loop $node_j$, j being an integer ≥ 1, according to the following rule:

- If the nodes $node_j$ and $node_{j-1}$ are part of a 2-block loop, then we will replace both the nodes by $\{(node_j)node_{j-1}\}$.

4.1. Algorithm for generating the PPC . Algorithm for generating the PPC for a given Program Tree Graph PTG:

- Step 1: PPC= 0, where 0 represents root node.
- Step 2: Modify PPC obtained above by replacing every node in PPC with its children, going from right to left in PTG, according to the following:

    1. If a child is a 2-block loop node, then insert the expansion of that child $\{node_j)node_{j-1}\}$.

    2. If a child is a loop $node_j$, then enclose that child by $\{node_j\}$.

    3. If a child is an n-component conditional node, then replace the child with its siblings that have the same local id and place them between delimiter pair ( ).

- Step 3: If every node in the list generated in the step above is a leaf, the list obtained is the PPC. If there is at least one node, which is not a leaf, go to step 2.

4.2. Example to generate PPC . Consider the program tree graph PTG in Fig. 3.1. For simplicity, we will replace node labels 2.1, 2.2, 2.3, 2.4, 2.5, 2.2.1, 2.2.2, 2.2.3 and 2.2.4 as follows:

$2.1 \Longrightarrow 5$

$2.2 \Longrightarrow 6$

$2.3 \Longrightarrow 7$

$2.4 \Longrightarrow 8$

$2.5 \Longrightarrow 9$

$2.2.1 \Longrightarrow 10$

$2.2.2 \Longrightarrow 11$

$2.2.3 \longrightarrow 12$

$2.2.4 \Longrightarrow 13$

We start with node 0. Hence $PPC_0 = 0$

We start by replacing the node by its children. Applying step 2 to PPC_0, we get

$PPC_1 = 1\{2\}3, 4.$

Next step 3 is applied. Since not every node in PPC_0 is a leaf node, we will go back to step 2, replacing the parents with their children. This gives

$PPC_2 = 1\{5(6, 7, 8)9\}3, 4.$

Not every node in PPC_2 is a leaf node. Observe that node 6 has children and hence node 6 is not a leaf node. Therefore, we go to step 2. Replace node 6 with its children. Hence, we have

$PPC_3 = 1\{5(< 10, (11, 12)13 > 7, 8)9\}3, 4.$

Now every node in PPC3 is a leaf node. Therefore,

PPC= $PPC_3 = 1\{5(< 10(11, 12)13 > 7, 8)9\}3, 4.$

5. Constructing the Execution Paths . The final step in estimating the WCET is to construct all possible paths a given program might take during execution.

DEFINITION 5.1. *When n-component conditional block reduction operation (defined below) is applied to PPC, we get a subset of PPC. If the operation is applied to a subset of PPC, we get a subset of this subset, which is also a subset of PPC.*

DEFINITION 5.2. *The following operation will be called n-component conditional block reduction:*

Suppose C is a PPC or a subset of PPC and has a n-component conditional block in it. Let there be x components in this block. Generate subset C_i, $1 \leq i \leq x$, from C in the following way:

$C_i = C$ in which the contents of the block are dropped and @component$_j$, $\forall j$, $1 \leq j \leq i$, from the original block is added to this new block. Each one of the newly formed lists Ci's gives a subset of the original PPC and is a cover of several paths or a path in the PTG. After adding all @component$_j$, $1 \leq j \leq i$, also add @component$_i$. Generate one more subset C_{i+1}, $C_{i+1} = C$ in which the contents of the group are dropped and @component$_i \forall i$, $1 \leq i \leq x$, is added to this group of the newly formed C_{i+1}.

5.1. Example of generating paths from n-component conditional block. Assume that we have the $PPC = 1(2, 3, 4, 5)6$. Observe that for the 4-component conditional block (2, 3, 4, 5), x=4. This generate 5 paths below:

$Path_1$= 1 2 6.

$Path_2$= 1 @2 3 6

$Path_3$= 1 @2 @3 4 6

$Path_4$= 1 @2 @3 @4 5 6

$Path_5$= 1 @2 @3 @4 @5 6

If x is equal to one, then a single a conditional block is encountered. If $x = 1$, create two lists C_1 and C_2. C_1 is a subset of C in which the contents of the group are unchanged. C_2 is a subset of C in which the contents of the group are dropped and @*component* is added.

If any one of the newly created subsets of PPC has an n-component conditional block in it, insert character $ at the end of the subset, implying that the subset is not a path but a cover for two or more paths. Such a cover of two or more paths will be denoted by $PathCover_j$, $j = 1$.

DEFINITION 5.3. *If the PPC contains a loop node, then an extra path is created to indicate the stopping condition of the loop. And that is accomplished by adding the @ symbol to the first node in the loop which is enclosed by '{' and '}' and dropping all the other nodes.*

5.2. Algorithm for generating the paths from a given PPC. In what follows, delimiters {} will be left in the resulting paths. However the delimiters () will be dropped. Scan, from left to right, the PPC or the subsets of PPC derived after the first iteration looking for an n-component conditional block and apply n-component conditional block reduction operation to the group just found and generate PPC subsets. If no such group is found, go to the next paragraph to deal with loop nodes. If an n-component conditional-group is found, repeat the procedure described in this paragraph.

If the PPC contains a loop node, then an extra path is created for the loop node to indicate the stopping condition of the loop. And that is accomplished by adding the @ symbol to the first node in the loop which is enclosed by '{' and '}' and dropping all the other nodes. When every loop node has been taken into account, we have the paths generated and the algorithm ends.

5.3. Example of generating paths . Consider the following PPC: $1\{5(< 10(11, 12)13 > 7, 8)9\}3, 4$

Delimiters {} will be left unchanged in the resulting paths. Scanning the PPC in the above example gives the following: (Note that $< 10(11, 12)13 >$ is selected while 7 and 8 are dropped. Add symbol $ at the end to indicate that this is a cover rather than a path since it includes a 2-component conditions block (11, 12).)

$PathCover_1 = \{5, 10(11, 12)13, 9\}3, 4\$$

Taking PathCover1 that has just been obtained, try to decompose it into paths by eliminating the delimiters (). In one path, we choose 11 to be part of it and in the other 12 is selected. Hence $PathCover_1$ yields two paths, $Path_1$ and $Path_2$.

$Path_1 = \{5, 10, 11, 13, 9\}3, 4$

$Path_2 = 1\{5, 10, @11, 12, 13, 9\}3, 4$

Now, going back to the PPC given and instead of selecting node $< 10(11, 12)13 >$ to be part of the path we drop it and select node 7. Since the nodes $< 10(11, 12)13 >$ are enclosed by ' <' and ' >', they will be treated as a single node. Since we are selecting node 7 to be part of the path, we drop $< 10(11, 12)13 >$ and add @10 to the path. Thus we get the following:

$Path_3 = 1\{5, @10, 7, 9\}3, 4$

Selecting node 8 gives the following path:

$Path_4 = 1\{5, @10, @7, 8, 9\}3, 4.$

The following is created to indicate that no iteration of the loop is to be taken:

$Path_5 = 1\{@5\}3, 4.$

6. Simulator Algorithm . The following algorithm computes the WCET for a given C program that is compiled into the assembly language of dual-pipeline processor. Whenever two adjacent instructions along a path are pairable and do not have data dependency as defined in section §2 above, they are paired to compute the time for simultaneous execution of the two instructions. Thus the time of execution of all instructions along a path is executed, pairing adjacent instructions whenever possible. This repeated for every path generated for the program. The algorithm assumes the following:

- The program for which WCET is to be computed is already compiled into assembly language of the target super-scalar processor and all possible program paths for the program have been generated and available in a set, called Set of Paths with p distinct paths,$p \geq 1$.
- The processor to be simulated has two pipelines, U and V.
- The rules for pairing are spelled out in a table, called Rule Table.
- The time for execution for each machine instruction is given in a table, called ET Table.
- The path to be tested in the simulator will be placed in Input Queue, which is fed to the simulator.
- $ExecTimeSum(i)$, $1 \leq i \leq p$, denotes the total time to execute all the instructions in the ith path being considered up-to but not including the 'current' instruction.

The following algorithm describes the simulation process applied to each program path in Set of Paths:

- Step 1: Set $i = 1$.
- Step 2: Place the sequence of instruction comprising path i in Set of Paths in Input Queue.
- Step 3: Set $ExecTimeSum(i) = 0$.
- Step 4: 'current' = the instruction at the head of the input sequence. 'next' = the instruction next to the instruction in 'current' in Input Queue.
- Step 5: If the instructions in 'current' and 'next' are pairable according to the rules in Rule Table, then check for data dependencies between the data of both instructions. If there are no data dependency then add the time to execute these two instruction in parallel to $ExecTimeSum(i)$ and drop both the instructions from Input Queue; otherwise add the execution time for only the instruction in 'current' to $ExecTimeSum(i)$ and drop the instruction in 'current' from Input Queue. If Input Queue is not empty, go to Step 4. If Input Queue is empty, increase i by 1. If $i > p$, the simulation for execution of all the paths in Set of Paths is completed; otherwise go to Step 2. Once the simulation is completed for all the paths in

the program, we can proceed to compute the worst case execution time as shown below:

$$WCET = max\{ExecTimeSum(i)\}.$$

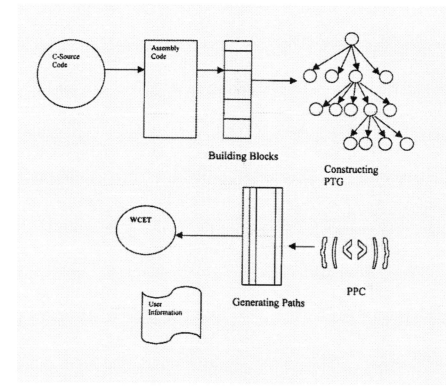

FIG. 7.1. *block diagram of the algorithm*

7. Implementation and Result. A prototype for the proposed algorithm has been implemented. Fig. 7.1 shows the block diagram of the algorithm. The prototype has been tested using C-based programs. In what follow, we examine the assembly code in Fig. 2.1.

The steps of generating the WCET path are highlighted in examples above. After examining the paths in the above examples , the WCET path is:

$1\{< 2.1, 2.2.1, 2.2.2, 2.2.4, 2.5, @2 >\}3, 4.$

The calculation of the WCET is shown Table 7.1. Table 7.1 shows the order of instructions that will execute in both pipelines. $\#CCn$ indicates the clock cycle for instruction n. A star next to the number in the total-cycle column indicates that both of the instructions in that line cannot be paired because of data dependency. The simulator gives accurate results of the pairing between instructions.

TABLE 7.1
WCET Calculation of a path.

Step	Instruction 1	pipe	#CC1	Instructions 2	pipe	#CC2	Total CC
0	push	UV	1	mov	UV	1	1
1	sub	UV	1	mov	UV	1	2
2	mov	UV	1	mov	UV	1	3
3	cmp	UV	2	jle	PV	1	5
4	mov	UV	1	cmp	UV	2	7
5	jne	PV	1				8
6	mov	UV	1	mov	UV	1	9
7	mov	UV	1	cmp	UV	2	11
8	jne	PV	1				12
9	mov	UV	1	mov	UV	1	13
10	jmp	PV	1				14
11	mov	UV	1	add	UV	2	15*
12	add	UV	2	mov	UV	1	17*
13	mov	UV	1	mov	UV	1	18
14	sub	UV	1	mov	UV	1	19*
15	mov	UV	1	jmp	PV	1	20
16	jmp	PV	1				21
17	cmp	UV	2	jle	PV	1	23
18	mov	UV	1	pop	UV	1	24
16	ret	NP	2				26

8. Conclusion. In this paper we have presented an assembly code-based method for calculating the WCET for a real-time system. In a dual-pipeline processor, two adjacent instructions may be executed simultaneously if they belong to pairable classes and do not have data dependency. We have introduced an algorithm that examines pairability of two adjacent instructions along a path which are not data dependent, and computes time of execution for every possible path. The algorithm utilizes a path generating approach to factor into the calculation the effects of super-scalar processor pipelining. Obtaining accurate estimates is cost-effective, since most of the real-time systems are embedded and are mass-produced. Also, an accurate estimate is an integral part in most of the scheduling algorithms, since they need to know the WCET of each task apriori. Currently, we are working to speed up the calculation process by generating fewer numbers of paths. Also we are working on an algorithm to enhance the detection of feasible paths.

REFERENCES

[1] C. LIU AND J. LAYLAND, *Scheduling algorithm for multiprogramming in a hard real-time environment*, Journal of the ACM, vol. 20, no. 1, pp. 46-61, Jan. 1973.
[2] S. LIM, Y. BAE, G.JANG, B. RHEE, S. MIN, C. PARK, H. SHIN, K. PARK, S. MOON AND C. KIM, *An Accurate Worst Case Timing Analysis for RISC Processors*, IEEE Transaction on Software Engineering, vol. 21, no. 7, pp. 593 -604, July 1995.
[3] D. NIEHAUS, *Program Representation and Translation for Predictable Real-time Systems*, Proceedings on 12th IEEE Real-Time Systems Symposium, pp 43-52, 1991.
[4] C. PARK AND A. SHAW, *Experiments with a Program Timing Tool Based on Source-Level*

Timing Schema, IEEE Computer. vol. 24, no. 5, pp. 48-57, May 1991.

[5] C. PARK, *Predicting Program Execution Times by Analyzing Static and Dynamic Program Paths*, Real-Time System. vol.5 ,no. 1, pp. 31-62, March 1993.

[6] P. PUSCHNER AND C. KOZA, *Calculating the maximum Execution Time of Real-Time Programs*, Real-Time Systems, vol. 1, no. 2, pp. 159-176, September 1989.

[7] M. HARMON, T. BAKER, AND D. WHALLEY, *A Retargetable Technique for Predicting Execution Time*, IEEE Real-Time Symposium, pp. 68-77, 1992.

[8] C. HEALY, R. ARNOLD, F. MUELLER, D. WHALLEY AND M. HARMON, *Bounding Pipeline and Instruction Cache Performance*, IEEE Transactions on Computers, vol. 48, no. 1, pp. 53-70, Jan. 1999.

[9] Y. LI AND S. MALIK, *Performance Analysis of Embedded Software Using Implicit Path Enumeration*, ACM SIGPLAN, vol. 30, pp. 88-98, Nov. 1995.

[10] A. MOK, *Evaluating Tight Execution Time Bounds of Programs by Annotations*, Proceedings of the 6th IEEE Workshop on Real-Time Operating Systems and Software, pp. 74-80, May 1989.

[11] N. ZHANG, A. BURNS AND M. NICHOLSON, *Pipelined processors and worst-case execution times*, Real-Time Systems, vol. 5, no. 4, pp. 319-343, Oct 1993.

[12] S. LIM, J. KIM, J. HAN AND S. MIN., *A worst case timing analysis technique for Multiple-Issue Machine*, Proceedings of the 19th IEEE Systems Symposium (RTSS98) Dec. 1998.

[13] J. CHOI, I. LEE AND I. KANG, *Timing analysis of super-scaler processor programs Using ACSR*, Proceedings of the 11th IEEE Workshop on Real-Time Operating Systems and Software, pp. 63-67, May 1994.

[14] E. HARCOURT, J. MAUNEY AND T. COOK, *High-level timing specification of instruction-level parallel processors*, Technical Report TR-93-18, Dept. of Computer Science, North Carolina State Univ., 1993.

INDEX